The Archetype
of the Unconscious
and the Transfiguration
of Therapy

The Archetype of the Unconscious and the Transfiguration of Therapy

Reflections on Jungian Psychology

Charles Poncé

North Atlantic Books
Berkeley, California

ISBN 1-55643-070-1

Published by
North Atlantic Books
2800 Woolsey Street
Berkeley, California 94705

Cover art by Ruth Terrill
Cover and book design by Paula Morrison
Typeset by Campaigne & Associates Typography

Printed in the United States of America

The Archetype of the Unconscious and the Transfiguration of Therapy is sponsored by the Society for the Study of Native Arts and Sciences, a nonprofit educational corporation whose goals are to develop an ecological and crosscultural perspective linking various scientific, social, and artistic fields; to nurture a holistic view of arts, sciences, humanities, and healing; and to publish and distribute literature on the relationship of mind, body, and nature.

For my son Jabir
on his twenty-first birthday

"And then went down to the ship . . ."

Acknowledgements

The greatest acknowledgement is to Phyllis, my wife, who has in her many readings, conversations, and fulminations consistently rescued this text from completely falling off its edge. I must also thank her for returning me to Bergson and bringing me to Deleuze. And to our children, Heather and Jabir, my love and appreciation for their patience with my long absences from the pleasure of their company this work demanded.

No work springs forth fully clad, but must instead dress and redress itself, practicing itself into a sensibility. There is no better arena for such preparations than the classroom and professional lecture-hall. There, ideas, theories, and imaginations may be subjected to the rigorous inspection of one's peers, and accordingly revised or aborted per the insights and intelligence they bring to them. Such opportunity has been graciously afforded me over the past ten or so years by the Pacifica Graduate Institute of Santa Barbara, and Rosebridge Graduate Institute of Walnut Creek. To the students and professionals of both these Institutions I extend my gratitude, and in particular to Tom Steele for his insightful comments on an earlier draft of this book.

To my publisher and friend, Richard Grossinger, my continued thanks for and respect of his dedication to the dissemination of ideas.

Finally, to Jacqueline McAbery, an unending thank you.

Contents

Part I

The
Penal
Colony

"The really scholarly people, the literary people, are the Egyptians, not the Greeks. What looks like learning among the Greeks originates among the Egyptians, and later returned home to blend its waters with the old current."

Nietzsche, *Notes for We Philologists*

"And since Egypt is the country where mythology places the origin of the gods, where the earliest observations of the stars are said to have been made, and where, furthermore, many noteworthy deeds of great men are recorded, we shall begin our history with the events connected with Egypt."

Diodoros, *History, I.9.5-6*

I must in the first Part of this work proceed slowly, in seeming mis-direction, opening avenues of inquiry usually foreign to the issues at hand. To discuss therapy it will first be necessary to investigate assumptions regarding the nature of the psyche and what we refer to as "psychological experience." It is to this end that the following pages will attempt to pry at the hermetic and hermeneutic seals created to encapsulate the ideas of subjectivity, interiority, and the unconscious.

This preliminary investigation will therefore not give the usual credence to concepts granted legitimacy solely because of their historicity or the prominence loaned them by the stature of previous investigators; it will concern itself with exploration and inquiry, not agreement and validation. My goal is one of inaugurating questions, of generating nomadic desires for the discovery of new sites where neither dialogue nor discourse gain prominence over simple inquiry. The fiction of answers I shall reserve for another work.

To arrive at a clearing where another type of speaking might occur, where investigation does not suffer the limitations of dialogue bound by consensuality (the unuttered strictures of tradition and propriety), it will first be necessary to clear the thick undergrowth of complacent acceptance that too often springs into the full bloom of certainty. Trees will sometimes need be felled as will rare species of bush and flower need be trampled. The swath will more often than not be one of broad machete-like strokes than of the gardener's pruning shears or the cautioned surgeon's scalpel. Time is of the essence, for the questions that should have been asked threaten soon to become blasphemous considerations, objects of ridicule or condemnation. An Inquisitorial mood presently settles like a fine dust on the linen of therapy.

Traditionally, it has been demanded of writers that if they should in the midst of their observations traverse the grain of established truths, marring the intellectual veneer of agreement, that they repair such damage *by returning to the site (at the very least) another sense of order. I shall not proceed in this manner, but will instead seek solely to open sites of further inquiry.*

This first Part that immediately follows should be understood as the glance that precedes all undertakings, the inhalation of beginnings. Read it with patience.

i.

If there is any legitimacy in turning to ancient cultures for insight into the operations of the psyche, we must base such inquiries upon lived experiences that are common to both the past and the present. Therefore, it is only by turning to natural phenomena that would have been seen by either primitive or ancient peoples as eternal and consistent in their presentation that we may on the one hand immediately experience their felt impression, and on the other investigate the conclusions that consciousness creates regarding such impression. It is only upon such participation with phenomena *as they are given* that we may in any manner presume that we understand not only the past, but the present.

There is no arguing that the impact of the experience natural phenomena give rise to are not the major concerns of everyday awareness. Most of us move through the world indifferent to not only the impact they have on us, but the results of such impact. We can assume that to a considerable extent such was also the case in ancient cultures. However, it would be foolhardy of us to think that the effect of these observations upon those few who so intensely observe, or who are driven by inner necessity to participate in experience to the point where they must philosophize, could account for the persistence of these ideas as established truths throughout the centuries. One can only hypothesize that, to the extent such perceptions became collectively meaningful explanations of some major aspect of everyday existence, they then became the imbedded ideas which constitute the internal dynamic of such social institutions as religion, philosophy, and science. It is through these vehicles that such ideas are transmitted from one generation to another. It is inevitable that the referent of their meanings would in time disappear, leaving us with nothing more than the institutional truths that the phenomenon had metamorphosized into, their original meaning lost.

Every natural phenomenon that stands out from the multitudinous backgrounds of existence, each delineated by its own phenomena—the heat and light of fire, the apparent rising and setting of the sun, the cyclical regularity of the seasons—will give rise to images which in any number of mythologies "intend" their meaning. We find an example of this in the depiction of the rising sun as an image of birth or rebirth. That the same image or symbol will be employed to convey the same idea in any number of diverse cultures across time does not necessarily indicate the existence of a racial or collective unconscious. One need not postulate the existence of a genetically transmitted archetypal-form residing in the human psyche, manifesting and making itself felt when prompted by human needs, to justify the ubiquity of these cultural images. Such conjectures have their origin in a deterministic metaphysic, an Idealism, the origins of which are the concerns of this work to the extent that it has infiltrated psychology—a branch of human inquiry whose stated obligation was the understanding of psychological phenomena and not simply an accommodation to and justification of them, and whose task was to have been participatory rather than regulatory.

What such cross-cultural imagery *does* indicate is that the psyche adopts and adapts itself to its apprehension of phenomena to create coded statements regarding its own existence. What the open eye and the apprehending sense experiences first is not the world but the certitude of its own presence which then extends into the world to include it as an object for itself, peripherally aware of a certainty that its "itself" would even be felt under the pitch-black dome of a Beckett night. If one must speak of a Logos it is this hyper-sensible response to phenomena that defines "being" under any condition of being. It is this Logos that stands over the creation of the person—the pliant bas-relief shaped and lifted (as a response) from the autonomous dispersion of experience organized and made meaningful by the community and the community of others.

What we are left with is the idea that the universality of images in the form of symbols occurs because of the manner by which consciousness is impacted on and apprehends phenomena, "internalizes" the apprehensions in accord with the group's agreed upon meaningful ontological answers, and then "externalizes" these answers as its own truth. Such truths in time become the objects of intellectual and/or metaphysical speculation and further differentiation, giving rise to doctrines that an entire group then identifies as its collective truth.

As for collective truth in general, Foucault tells us it is the product of power, "produced only by virtue of multiple forms of constraint . . . [inducing] regular effects of power."[1] It is, as Foucault stresses, neither achieved nor rewarded but given as a society's "'general politics' of truth," a regime that determines

> ". . . the types of discourse which it accepts and makes function as true; the mechanisms and instances which enable one to distinguish true and false statements, the means by which each is sanctioned; the techniques and procedures accorded value in the acquisition of truth; the status of those who are charged with saying what counts as true."[2]

Of the many vehicles by which truth is transmitted, held up as inviolable, one which will concern us is the story—for power's manner of self-validation is its very personification.[3] By such personification power enters into the field of everyday actors, originating itself in the realm of the human and the personal, arranging social life along the guidelines of its own index. There, in the story, power may not only be readily "understood," but legitimating (by claiming that its origin was but the result of specific types of human interaction, and not just simply a social or political formula for the distribution of rights). The power of the "truth" is conveyed by the dramatic activities and events played out by the characters composing the story. Thus, the "truth" of Christianity is presented us in the story—from birth to death—of the Christ. It is the story

---

[1]Michel Foucault, *Power/Knowledge*, New York: Pantheon Books, 1980, p. 131.

[2]*Ibid*.

[3]Throughout this work I will employ the term "story" in its fictive sense only, as that which is feigned, modeled in clay (from the Latin *fingere*), and therefore imagined and invented. Whenever I seek to address or discuss that which is (to all appearances) a true accounting of things, I will use the term "history."

that allows the "general politics of truth" to maintain itself as public knowledge on the one hand, and (via its dramatic and emotional imagery) impact and organize the psyche within the limits of its parameters—each element acting as a station along the lifespan of (as we shall see) a Western *via negativa*.

The story of an existing tradition is always presented as history —its effectiveness as a social directive and shaper (along with its longevity) indicating the magnitude of its power as truth. For most of us in the West, the stories of the Judeao-Christian tradition are an immediate example. The recent and continuing controversies concerning the teaching of Biblical history as an alternative to Darwinism reached even the Supreme Court (a social institution called upon to judge its own cultural institution along judicial lines parented by Greek and not Hebraic law). But we must also attend to the fact that many elements in most traditional religious histories when surveyed by a non-believer are understood as fictive in that they defy empirical reality. If the believer is aware of such difficulties, he will often inform us that the discrepancy is resolved through the machinery of metaphor, symbolism, and in the final analysis pure faith in the story as truth.

In the presence of a living religion we are immediately faced with the power of a truth carried by its story. What we "understand" of the story is not its literary or symbolic meaning, the fabrication of stories out of fiction (a polytheism of monotheism), but the power of the truth that the story portrays. This understanding is a *felt* experience that touches both our personal and social lives, creating a meaning whose validity is measured by its acceptance among those who are socially significant to us. Once this felt experience is no longer conveyed by the story, then (in the case of religion) we are in the presence of a mythology. If there is to be numinosity it will be found in that which cannot be found—the politics of truth that the stories originally conveyed, the imbedded values that the culture has aestheticized into metaphors immediately recognizable within its milieu's setting. It is only when the original referent is lost that we can truly begin to speak of these images as symbols, as mythologems. The category "mythology" simply refers us to a religion that is no longer collectively or personally viable. Matters become even more complicated when a transmigration of symbols occurs—when a symbol from one culture is appropriated by another culture. In time the fact of such cultural "borrowings" or appropriations itself becomes lost.

ii.

Of course to discuss in what manner the "internalization" of natural phenomena becomes the *prima mobilia* of religion and psychology it will be necessary to converse within the parameters of a mythology. For this task none is better suited than the mythology of Egypt. In the first place, it did not undergo the splintering and differentiation that the aesthetic and philosophical traditions of Greek culture brought to their own mythology. Aesthetics—aside from the license it allows the artist to depart from facticities—serves itself first, and attends to phenomenal reality later, if at all. In the second place, Egyptian mythology essentially concerned itself with the answer to one major ontological question—what is death? The directness with which it approached this one question offers us a reasonably uncluttered picture of how consciousness greets and assembles its experience of this inevitability. In contrast, the philosophic and aesthetic approach to phenomena, along with the myriad ontological questions Greek culture addressed, has left us with an inheritance of problems and complexities open to a universe or more of interpretations.

It was out of the Egyptians' single and focused concern with death that many of our ideas regarding the nature of the soul, rebirth, heaven, hell, conscience, and the after-life more than likely have their origin in the Western World. Too often we overlook the impact Egypt had on the Greek world, especially when the latter is presented as the root of European culture. The textual legacy of Egyptian culture is more consistent and complete than that offered us in the fragments of Greek civilization simply because it rarely came under the hand of the individual artisan. It consistently expressed a collective and constant belief. In addition, the geographical realities of Egyptian civilization caused certain types of natural phenomena to be impressed starkly upon the Egyptian mind—the most immediate of which was the horizon.

The horizon is a visible and immediate line of demarcation that always stands in front and behind the human world, out of reach. It is this out-of-reachedness, its existence as a locale whose other side can never be crossed, that also gives rise to the idea of an other-side that is invisible. It exists in an atemporal and aspatial reality, as an essence or a signification. Thus, the image of the invisible is perpetually and visibly present: the horizon is proof of its existence, our inability to transgress it its fact.

In the phenomenon of the horizon we are presented with the idea that a thing can exist without formal being, that cannot be traversed by existence, the other-side of which is a place of non-being. It is eternally before us, neither receding nor advancing, situating us at center. It is from this perpetual placement at center that human beingness originally acted, identifying itself with the divinity it would eventually assign to the Pole and circumpolar stars that seemingly turn about it eternally. In much the same way that the horizon of the world is a dimension that cannot be stepped over, so too must we recognize that the world itself, in its entirety, in that we experience it as a phenomenal reality, is an horizon. To step beyond the experience of this world is to die. Because all experience, even experience of transcendence, occurs within *this* phenomenal world, we could therefore say that to have an horizon is to have being. The horizon defines our existence but is never located in the midst of our existence, and its invisible other-sided-ness is felt as a presence and a force, mysterious in its paradoxical presence and non-presence. This feeling is punctuated by the appearance of phenomena as eternal and mysterious as the horizon itself.

What we do see of the other side of the horizon is also beyond our reach, perfect in its daily and nightly presentation: the astronomical heavens. It is at the horizon where we see the sun rise in the East, traverse the sky, disappear, only to re-emerge again in the West. In a social world of inconsistency, we can be assured of the eternally consistent. All of the sun's eternal activities occur on "the other side" of the horizon, in that realm from which we are excluded. Furthermore, the activities of this star inform us that the other side has an equally inaccessible "under" to it through which (we are forced to imagine by the reasonable-ness of what is presented) it travels from the time of its Western descent to that of its Eastern ascent. It is the experience of the horizon line that therefore gives birth to the division of the world into an above and a below—the below being but another aspect of the inaccessible presence of the other-side.

Thus, the horizon not only gives birth to the idea of a dimension we as living beings never reach, but also to an under-the-horizon dimension that can never be seen. To journey there is to experience what the sun must surely experience each night—a death.[4] To the ancient mind this underworld of the horizon was the land of the dead, of spirits, and divine powers. It is in this manner that the phenomenon of the horizon first gave rise to the idea of another world or province of activity greater than our own.

iii.

What is not understood becomes divinized; the numinosity of the unthought thought gathers to itself the operations of the human world to explain what it cannot understand except through a doubling operation.[5] The microcosm gives birth to the macrocosm to explain its own origin. The fictive is the mirror by which humanity gazes at itself, finding justification for its actions—justifying itself to itself. Such legitimations are the stuff of certainty. It is in this aspect that we meet the story of the horizon in Egyptian religion:

> "When Nephthys gave birth to Anubis, Isis treated the child as if it were her own; for Nephthys is that which is beneath the Earth and invisible, Isis that which is above the earth and visible; *and the circle which touches these, called the horizon, being common to*

---

[4]Budge informs us that the Sun god Ra when he passes out of daytime, over the horizon, becomes the sun god of the night, Af, "represented with the head of a ram surmounted by a solar disk." E. A. Wallis Budge, *The Gods of the Egyptians*, New York: Dover Publications, Inc., 1969, Vol. I, p. 206.

[5]The best analysis to date of this doubling operation, based upon resemblance as a category of thought, its four differentiating principles of *convenientia, aemulatio, analogy, and sympathies* articulating the body of the universe, is to be found in Foucault's meticulous presentation in his *The Order of Things: An Archeology of the Human Sciences*, New York: Vintage Books, 1973, pp. 17-30.

both, has received the name Anubis, and is represented in form like a dog; for the dog can see with his eyes both by night and by day alike."[6]

Nephthys represented death and the underworld, whereas Isis stood for birth and the upper world of life.[7] The child that they share in common, Anubis, was a jackal god who prowled the precinct of the tombs, the places of the dead—those who had passed "to the other side." He was the product of the union of Nephthys with her brother Osiris, the God of light. What we must take note of here is that whereas the horizon of the everyday world does not and cannot give birth to the reality of another side or a beyond (one can never get to, cross over or go past the horizon), the designation of the "other side" in terms of its representing death and the beyond is what gives birth to an eschatology. The other side of the horizon is imagined as a world beyond this world. The tale also informs us that it is the underworld, the death-realm, that gives birth to the horizon. Thus we should not be too surprised to find that the horizon has qualities normally assigned to the underworld—inaccessibility, invisibility, and numinosity. Its mother is death, its aunt life.

The name "Anubis" is the Greek for the Egyptian word *Anpu.* The verb *anp* means "to wrap around," and refers us to the embalmers' wrapping of the mummy with bandages. If Anubis is the horizon that is "wrapped" around the whole of humanity, and to be alive is to be contained by an horizon, then the bandages as horizon-markers refer us to the theme of immortality that runs throughout the course of Egyptian religion. The identification of the body *with* the horizon-bandage, established by its immediate proximity to the body suggests that the deceased was no longer subject to the demarcating dimensions of this world. A new space was entered where horizon and body become one. The interpretation of the horizon as a synonym for eternal life extends to the

---

[6]Frank Cole Babbitt, trans., *Plutarch's Moralia,* Cambridge, Massachusetts: Harvard University Press, 1969, vol. 5, para. 368e. My emphasis.

[7]Budge, *Gods,* vol. II, p. 258.

11

tomb itself which is referred to as "the eternal horizon."[8] A pyramid therefore signifies an horizon and was seen by the Egyptians as an horizon contained *within* an horizon. But here an inverse relationship between person and horizon occurred: in the presence of a pyramid the living person existed *outside* of an horizon, meaning that he was actively present to the mystery of the "other-side." The transmundanality of what the pyramid represented became geographically situated in much the same manner that the center of the world in all cultures becomes geographically located. Thus, the world in the *Old Testament* is located away from the centrally positioned East of Eden—a garden one cannot any more enter than one can the sanctity of the pyramid-tomb.

In short, all divine space is demarcated by an horizon line. By designating the pyramid as an horizon that exists within the world rather than circumscribing the world, the Outside (that which is beyond the immediately perceivable world of phenomena) becomes located in the inside. That is, the Outside of the inside is greater and more extensive than the inside itself. One can say that the Outside has been folded or invaginated to create an inside which it now co-exists with. We shall see that this fold is one of four necessary for the creation of the experience of subjectivity.[9]

From this we can see that it is the nature of the psyche to have structure assigned to it through an identification of its experience with geographical reality, by a folding of the Outside. But what we call an identification is actually an *act of determination* on the psyche's part to organize itself topologically around meaning-structures in an attempt to comprehend its experience of the phenomenal world. An identification is an act of determination in

---

[8]Cf. the administrative accounting of the Pyramids in 115 B.C. and its reference to the tomb of King Amenophis I in, Ange-Pierre Leca, *The Cult of the Immortal*, London: Granada Publishing Limited, 1982, p. 207.

[9]Here I follow Deleuze's systematisation of Foucault's analysis in *The Use of Pleasure*, New York: Vintage Books, 1986, pp. 25-32, in Gilles Deleuze, *Foucault*, Minnesota: University of Minnesota Press, 1988, p. 104. The four folds are ". . . the material part of ourselves . . . the fold of the relation between forces . . . the fold of knowledge . . . [and] the fold of the outside itself, the ultimate fold." *ibid.*, p. 104. I will address the constitution and problem of the fourth fold in Part II of this work.

that by it "I" seek to define myself not by subjective considerations, but by a seemingly meaningful relationship between myself and an object other than myself. It is by such relationship that the experience of subjectivity begins to take shape. The structuring of a "myself" (in the modern Western World) by such identification is present in infancy and remains as an active dynamic of the psyche throughout our lives.

Much the same thing occurs with the location of the "upper" in or on the "lower" by the Egyptians' projection of celestial bodies onto the landscape. We therefore discover that the sequence of the Zodiacal Egyptian animals was replicated in the townships along the portion of the Nile in Upper Egypt.[10] In other words, there is not just simply a correspondence between the upper and the lower, the macrocosm with the microcosm, there is a locating of the upper *with* the lower, thereby making the lower coextensive with the upper. Yet another folding by which the lower shares the limitless space of the other-side.

By its affiliation with death the horizon, the moving edge of the world, reflects the moveable edge of the social world, the edge of the community to which the unexplainable is exiled. It is here where those who deal with other-side issues (which as we shall see are identified with the divine) are socially identified and located. This Outside of the damned and divine is the location of the scapegoat in Western culture. The peculiarity of the space shared by corpse and embalmer is unusual in that its spiritual distinction is marked by its exclusion from the social.

In Egyptian culture this was the domain of those who were identified with and served Anubis—the embalmers, who by contract were limited to specific geographical areas and responsible for the dead from their assigned villages. The office of embalmers was hereditary, but of considerable low rank in the social hierarchy. The embalmers were held in both awe and disgust by the general population: a special decree had to be passed during the Ptolemaic period to protect them from expulsion and open harassment by

---

[10]Harald A. T. Reiche, "The Language of Archaic Astronomy: A Clue to the Atlantis Myth?," in Kenneth Brecher & Michael Feirtag, editors, *Astronomy of the Ancients,* Cambridge: The MIT Press, 1981, p. 175.

the general public. However, within the vicinity of their own workspace they were treated as if they were the gods themselves:

> "'Anubis, Overseer of the Mysteries' directed operations wearing a jackal-head mask which represented the god who had presided over the embalming of Osiris. The 'Chancellor of the gods,' who from the Sixth Dynasty onwards was the chief embalmer, assisted him and played the role of Horus, son of Isis and Osiris. They were surrounded by readers, priests whose task it was to recite the liturgies while the different stages of mummification were being carried out. No doubt it also devolved on them to choose the wrappings and draw the ritual figures on the linen."[11]

It is important to note that in the past the excluded was not only identified with the spiritual or divine, but also with the therapeutic.[12] We find that as late as the Fifth Century B.C. annually, on the 6th day of Thargelion, the city of Athens chose one man and one woman as *pharmakoi*, scapegoats, who where then led out beyond the city walls and stoned to death. These victims were selected from "a number of degraded and useless beings [maintained] at the public expense; and when any calamity, such as plague, drought, or famine befell the city, they sacrificed two of these scapegoats."[13]

The spiritualization of the outcast is the manner by which a collective body normalizes itself, i.e., "heals" itself of disorder. That which is unacceptable becomes an "other-world" issue and an object of "inverse exaltation."[14] The excluded is *given* the socially proper perspective—as one who has been elected to serve a social purpose. The existing regime of truth determines whether

---

[11] Ange-Pierre Leca, *Cult*, pp. 143-4.

[12] As Foucault reminds us such "rigorous division which is social exclusion but spiritual regeneration," became medically organized during the Middle Ages when the leprosariums housed those whose disease was diagnosed as an example of God's power of damnation. Leprosy was therefore a divine disease, and the leper stood forth as an example of divinity's wrath. cf. Michel Foucault, *Madness and Civilization*, New York: Vintage House, 1973, pp. 6, 7.

[13] Sir James Frazer, *The Golden Bough*, New York: The Macmillan Company, 1958, p. 670.

[14] Foucault, *Madness*, p. 6.

such election is spiritual, psychological, or criminal. What I am attending to here is that the act of election raises the excluded to a special status, and that such status is of a *religious* nature simply because of the individual's socially "exalted" position.

The willingness with which individuals often purposively offered themselves as scapegoats, knowing that at the end of a specific term they would either be killed or exiled, is but an indication of the "spirituality" assigned to such offices.[15] The value and rewards given to those who fulfill the office of scapegoat in the Western World are fully visible in the image of the tale of the personification of the Christ as the Judaic paschal lamb. The degree to which the Christian affords value to the Imitation of Christ as a path of redemption is the degree to which the individual is *himself* a voluntary scapegoat. It must be added that as in other situations of reverse exaltation, the Christ was also both a redeemer and a *pharmakon*:

> "One of Augustine's favorite images for church leaders, as for their model, Christ, is that of the physician, ministering to those who have been baptized but, like himself, are still sick, each one infected with the same ineradicable disease contracted through original sin. Augustine tends, consequently, to discount the patients' opinions. It is the physicians' responsibility not only to administer to sick and suffering humanity the life-giving medication of the sacraments, but also to carry out, when necessary, disciplinary procedures as a kind of surgery."[16]

All of this will become even more relevant to our inquiry when we discuss the figure of the twentieth-Century patient of the therapeutic encounter.

The place of the excluded is also the place of judgement, for we are told that Anubis—the personification of the horizon—assays the heart of the deceased, "emblematic of the conscience, [which]

---

[15]Sir James Frazer, *Golden Bough*, Chapter LVII, "Public Scapegoats," pp. 651-658, and Chapter LVIII, "Human Scapegoats in Classical Antiquity," pp. 669-679.

[16]Elaine Pagels, *Adam, Eve, and the Serpent*, New York: Random House, 1988, p. 117. Here I would turn the reader's attention to the image of the Wounded Healer that several contemporary therapies align themselves with.

is to be weighed in the Balance against the ostrich feather, emblematic of 'law,' 'truth,' etc."[17] That is to say, judgement and law operate within the vicinity of an horizon where they attain their numinosity because of their concern with the over-the-horizon issues of exclusion and exile. The measurement was performed to insure that the individual had the right to enter into the presence of Osiris, a judgement which demanded that he had always:

a. Spoken the truth.

b. Brought no harm to "any man by word or deed."[18]

c. Strictly observed the rule of honesty in handling the properties of either gods or men.

d. Made sure to commit no sins against the gods, always protecting their dignity and guarding their sacred precincts.

> "It is clear that what Osiris abominated above all other things were lying, prevarication, deceit, and insincerity. To him the speaker of crooked words must necessarily be a doer of crooked deeds, and the proof of this fact is the words *maat kheru*, 'whose word is truth,' which it was the proud hope of every Egyptian to have applied to him by Thoth, by the gods, and by Osiris himself, the God of Truth."[19]

Failing any of these laws, the individual's heart (which contained his *ka*, his double or abstract personality) was given over to the Eater of the Dead who sat near the Balance.[20]

The Egyptian identification of subjective experiences of the heart with the *ab* soul is but one example of the idea that the gods could be identified with internal body organs. In *The Book of the Dead*, we find the following reference:

> "Thou [my heart] art my Ka, the dweller in . . . my body, the god Khnemu who makest sound my members."[21]

---

[17]E. A. Wallis Budge, *The Book of the Dead*, New Hyde Park, New York: 1960, p. 234.

[18]*Ibid.*, p. 239.

[19]*Ibid.*, p. 239.

[20]*Ibid.*, p. 237.

[21]*Ibid.*, pp. 339-40.

In other words, by the body's housing of the gods in the form of its own organs it too became divinized. In much the same manner that the folding of the horizon onto the enclosure of the social world brought about a condition of spiritual and spatial co-extensiveness, so too does the identification of body organs with deity make the interior of the body coextensive with the cosmos and its powers. The gods could therefore be experienced as subjective realities—if not of emotions themselves, then most certainly as their source. The divinities of the other-side, the Outside, penetrate and become located in the human body via the identification of its organs with the gods. The heart, or *ab*, was not only the seat of conscience, but the organ through which "wish, longing, desire, lust, will, courage, mind, wisdom, sense, intelligence, manner, disposition, attention, intention, etc." originated.[22] In short, the heart was thought of as the seat of all consciousness and emotion. A similar belief prevailed in Greek culture during Homeric times.[23]

What we see in such mortuary judgements—in all cultures, and not just Egypt—are the ethical, moral, and social values (the norm) of the group performing the funerary ritual. Funerary rituals reflect social expectations regarding the fulfillment of an ideal.

iv.

W.B. Kristensen noted that to the Egyptian mind the alternation of day and night did not signify a displacement or death of either phenomenon, but rather a situation in which one takes refuge in the other:

> "In this, attention was naturally concentrated on the two points where the hostile powers meet and combine, that is, the eastern and western horizons. Both harbor the same mystery and are therefore regarded as points of precisely the same character. The two horizons were viewed as essentially identical; what applied

---

[22]E. A. Wallis Budge, *Osiris & the Egyptian Resurrection*, New York: Dover Publications, Inc, 1973, vol. II, pp. 130-1.

[23]Richard Broxton Onians, *The Origins of European Thought*, New York: Arno Press, 1973, pp. 40, 56, 171.

to one held true for the other too. That they were geographically separated could not obliterate the impression. In mythical cosmography they often assume one another's functions. The place where the light sets is also called the place where it rises . . ."[24]

Kristensen later refers us to a description of a votive pyramid on which the side depicting the West, or region of the setting and dying sun, also has inscribed on it the hieroglyph for the god who represents resurrection and the rising sun, Khepera. As he observes, "This implies a conception of the Western horizon and of what is happening there at sunset which cannot be expressed in rational terms."[25] The Western horizon, always (and in all mythologies) associated with death and the underworld, is also in Egyptian religion the place where the sun returns to life. The meaning of cyclical renewal—of life out of death in the phenomena of the seasons, the seeming death of insects and creatures who disappear into hibernation at the time of the settling and dissipation of the Nile's waters, the nightly return of human life out of the darkness of sleep into the light of daytime consciousness—depended upon a religious belief that the oppositional conditions of phenomena were ultimately resolved by their congenial fusion. The Eastern and Western horizon become the same horizon by a folding. As in our earlier discussion regarding the pyramids as horizons and the establishment of an Outside in an inside, of the divinity of the other-side becoming located in the inner world of society (as well as in the body), so too here do we find a rationalization that the phenomena occurring at geographical points reveal the topology of an other dimension. The horizons that define my experience of dying and being reborn, of going to sleep and waking up, are one and the same. As an ancient Egyptian, what I experience of my own daily becoming not only occurs *in* Nature, but also predates, blueprints, and constructs my own nature. As the world, so too do I have an horizon over which I nightly step. The body of the world and our bodies, and the dimension of an other world overlap. It is in this overlap where I experience what I then come to

---

[24]quoted in N. Rambova, "The Symbolism of the Papyri," in Alexandre Piankoff, trans., N. Rambova, editor, *Mythological Papyri*, New York: Pantheon Books, 1957, vol. 3, Part I, p. 29.

[25]*Ibid.*, p. 30.

believe is a major determining feature of the invisible and the visible: that they are complementary, and that their differences may be best described in terms of what is "inner" and "outer,"—synonyms for the divine and the mundane, form and matter, unconsciousness and consciousness. The horizon-lines of coming-to-be and passing-away, being the same, find imitation in the demarcating line between consciousness and the unconscious. This is further illustrated by a description of the physical and divine aspects of the sun god Ra as he enters into the realm of the Western Mountain, the invisible land of the underworld: "Come to us, He who rows his Flesh [the body of Re]. . . . The sky is for thy soul, the earth for thy body."[26]

In Egyptian religion, during the time of the Pyramid texts (*circa* 2425-2300 B.C.) the underworld, or Tuat, was located in the Northern portion of the sky, in the region of the circumpolar stars that never set, and which the Greeks would in time refer to as the location of their undying gods.[27] What has been translated as the "underworld" for this period of Egyptian history actually refers us to the Northern heavens, and not a domain located under the earth.[28] The location of dead souls was, properly speaking, an invisible domain existing in the sky, symbolized by the circumpolar stars. It was with the later spread of the spiritual significance given to the sun that the land of the dead shifted to a location under the earth—not contained *in* the earth, but in the Southern hemisphere of the sky. Thus, as I alluded to earlier, the sky is the other side, and the *under* of the horizon line is not only "the invisible" but that which is without flesh, without physical substance. The mummy is referred to as "Image of Flesh,"[29] which on the one hand suggests the Egyptian belief that the deceased was on his way to becoming the god, and on the other reveals that this description of the folding of the visible onto the invisible is the way

[26]*Ibid.*, p. 37.

[27]H. Frankfort, H. A. Frankfort, J. A. Wilson, T. Jacobsen, *Before Philosophy*, Baltimore, Maryland: Penguin Books, 1963., p. 57.

[28]E. A. Wallis Budge, *The Egyptian Heaven & Hell*, La Salle, Illinois: Open Court, p. 88.

[29]Rambova, "Symbolism," p. 37.

in which the psyche universally describes its embodied presence to itself. Thus do we find the *Old Testament* also stating that the human race was made in "the image of God." That is, the human body is a corporeal image, a representation of the divine, of form and essence combined.

So now we have a second folding. The first fold was of geographical position, whereas this second concerns itself with the body. The first fold gave rise to a self existing within a "within."[30] The second, to a defining of the "without" that the body is, and which contains a spiritual or psychological "within." It was the Greeks who would bring emphasis to a third fold.

The object of the Greek fold was neither geographic, astronomic, nor concrete, but instead the abstract phenomenon of the force of power. Because force can only exist in relation to another force, this folding operation created a relation to oneself based upon self-mastery, a condition in which force relates to itself.[31] This self-mastery came about through the subjectiviation of the Platonic model of the ideal Republic which would be constructed and governed along the lines of the tripartite soul and ruled by a Philosopher-King. This third fold is the place where, "the relation between forces is bent back in order to become a relation to oneself."[32] What became folded were the relationships of power as they appear in society.

V.

Almost all of the pre-Socratics thought of the universe as a quasi-living organism, a world-soul whose full ethical and psychological dimensions did not become completely formalized until Plato, in his *Timaeus*, defined it as the creator of all orderly motion in the universe. With the aid of the inclusion of Babylonian astronomical records, and the mathematical formulations that grew out of such observation, Plato not only shifted the image of

---

[30]Deleuze, *Foucault*, p. 114.

[31]*Ibid.*, p. 97ff, and Michel Foucault, *The Use of Pleasure*, New York: Vintage Books, pp. 25-32.

[32]Deleuze, *Foucault*, p. 104.

the soul from the realm of the Socratic personal to the cosmic and transpersonal, but showed that the eternal and orderly movements of the stars were the product of a rational mind:

"The whole course and motion of Heaven and all it contains have a motion like to the motion and revolution and reckonings of reason."[33]

That is, Plato proposed the existence of a cosmic consciousness that creates a mathematical orderliness in all things, its dynamic and animating force being the soul. This mathematization of the cosmos (an intimation of Galileo's later mathematization of Nature) gave us the image of a mathematical and ordering logos.[34] We are further told that it is number itself that gives the human race its reason, if not its consciousness, by a god that may be called either Cosmos, Olympus, or Uranus, and whose presence allows the soul to attain its virtue and its perfect goodness, for number is the source of all good things.[35] It is the soul and its affiliation with number, the logos of the universe, that holds up to us the promise of perfection wherein is contained all wisdom and virtue. This cosmological image is given to us as the standard by which we can begin to discuss the ideal norm we all should in some manner or another attempt to emulate.[36] In Plato's mind, every soul has been impaired, wounded by its birth in the human body, and in immediate need.

"As concerning the most sovereign form of soul in us we must conceive that heaven has given it to each man as a guiding genius—that part which we say dwells in the summit of our body and lifts us from earth towards our celestial affinity, like a plant whose roots are not in earth, but in the heavens. . . . The

---

[33]Laws, 897c, quoted in S. Sambursky, *The Physical World of the Greeks*, Princeton: Princeton University Press, 1987, p. 68.

[34]Edith Hamilton and Huntington Cairns, editors, *The Collected Dialogues of Plato*, Princeton, New Jersey: Princeton University Press, 1973, *Epinomis*, 978b,c. All references to Plato will be to this edition unless otherwise indicated. For Galileo's mathematization of Nature I refer the reader to Edmund Husserl's *The Crisis of European Sciences*, David Carr, trans., Evanston: Northwestern University Press, 1970, pp. 23-59.

[35]*Ibid.*, 978a.

[36]*Ibid.*, 978c-e. Also see, Francis Macdonald Cornford, *Plato's Cosmology*, London/New York: Routledge & Kegan Paul, 1971, pp. 74-93.

motions akin to the divine part in us are the thoughts and revolutions of the universe; these, therefore, every man should follow,
and correcting those circuits in the head that were deranged at
birth, by learning to know the harmonies and revolutions of the
world . . ."[37]

Thus, every individual bears within himself a deranged consciousness that must be realigned. Here lies the basic premise of
depth psychology—that there are resolutions and redemptions
the psyche must undergo if it is again to achieve the orderly operations of a normal and complete soul—such operations in the final
analysis (in the Twentieth Century) measurable by statistical determinations, psychological testing, and the poetic license of differential diagnosis. This premise echoes Plato's mathematization of both
the cosmos and man, leading us toward a similar echo regarding
his Ideas and Jung's theory of the archetypes of the collective
unconscious; they too are described as answering to a drummer
as distant as the pre-Hellenic *Nike*.

It was for the correction of the pathology created by the fold
of the macrocosm into the microcosm that Plato proposed the creation of therapy. Thus it is that in his *Phaedrus* he creates the art
of differential diagnosis, explaining that the healer of soul must
first determine the various possible infirmities of the soul. Only
then may the practitioner choose the appropriate healing speech.[38]
It is imperative that we take note of the Platonic statement that no
one is born without the deranged circuitry of the injured soul, for
it informs us that any who approach a healer will be assumed
wanting not simply because of his approach, but because of an
innate and inherent condition. To access one's true soul, one must
first recognize themselves as a patient. Furthermore, in that the
circuitry of our minds is the product of the orderly expression of
the gods, the mind is the province and property of religion.

Collective religion in Greece had always been a matter of the
state or polis; the favor of the gods sought by official priests was
for the community and not for the souls of the citizens. "The state
religion was therefore perfunctory, not evangelical,"[39] "not tuned

---

[37]*Timaeus*, 90a,c,d, trans. in *Ibid.*, pp. 353, 354.

[38]Plato, *Phaedrus*, 271b, ff.

[39]cf. Finley Hooper, *Greek Realities: Life and Thought in Ancient Greece*,
Detroit: Wayne State University Press, 1978, p. 387.

to the religious needs of the individual; it shapes the community of the polis, pointing out and verbalizing its functions through its gods."[40] In the midst of all this a popular religion, composed of cults devoted to this or that God or Goddess, always existed. These cults were initially of a private and elite nature—the responsibility of an aristocracy composed of warriors and priests. Such had been the case, for example, with the Eleusinian cult which throughout the centuries up to its close relied upon the offices of two families. The Hierophant, or high priest of the Mysteries, was drawn from the family of the Eumolpidai, the Dadouchos, or "torch-bearer" from the family of the Kerykes.[41]

The hold of popular religion on the Greek mind had been considerably undermined by the establishment of the *polis*, the city, and its laws. Once these laws were written down for the citizens to read, the sacraments which once had been under the sole authority of the king suddenly became the property of the common person. The work of *Dike* (Justice) was no longer a secret held in the hands of the few. It still existed in a sovereign, divine, distant, and inaccessible realm, but now stood over both sovereign and citizen alike. Whenever the fabric of a traditional cosmogony begins to fade in this manner an ethic following philosophical lines eventually emerges.[42] Philosophy, which had been the province of the intellectual aristocracy, now approached the general public where it sought to fill the space left by religion's collapse. It actively proselytized through the agencies of public literary tracts, classes of instruction, and sermons, and began to influence public opinion in a manner never before known, the Epicureans and Stoics holding the greatest influence.

It was with the advent of the Hellenistic schools of this period that individualism and the concept of the person became the focus of philosophy. Whereas Plato and Aristotle had petitioned that the polis be self-sufficient, these schools turned self-sufficiency into a

---

[40]Walter Burkert, *Greek Religion,* Cambridge: Harvard University Press, 1985, p. 335.

[41]Carl Kerenyi, *Eleusis: Archetypal Image of the Mother and Daughter,* New York: Pantheon Books, 1967, p. 23.

[42]cf. Arthur W. H. Adkins, *Merit and Responsibility: A Study in Greek Values,* Oxford: Clarendon Press, 1960.

basic attribute of the individual.[43] The creation of the self-sufficient individual was given further delineation by the Greek idea of a Natural Law:

> "Its leading idea is the idea of God as the universal, spiritual-and-physical, Law of Nature, which rules uniformly over everything and as universal law of the world orders nature, produces the different positions of the individual in nature and in society, and becomes in man the law of reason which acknowledges God and is therefore one with him. . . . The Law of Nature thus demands on the one hand submission to the harmonious course of nature and to the role assigned to one in the social system, on the other an inner elevation above all this and the ethico-religious freedom and dignity of reason, that is one with God and therefore not to be disturbed by any external or sensible occurrence."[44]

It was from this thesis that "the concept of an ethical law of nature from which are derived all juridical rules and social institutions,"[45] a creation of the Stoics, became the cornerstone of the Western World's construction of a social reality that is presently authenticated by psychology.

The collapse of a cosmogony at first sight appears to release the person from all transcendent indenture, moving him along in an orderly fashion towards rationalism. The complaint since the end of the Nineteenth Century is that the West has become *too* rational, *too* scientific, because it has left behind the religious and metaphysical truths that had guided it in the past. Such is not the case, however: whereas the belief of the Gods has been put aside, the moral imperatives ingrained in the mythical cosmologies they embodied have not. The accusation of irreligiosity is heard loudest during the times of greatest spirituality, of transition away from one type of idolization to another, and the establishment of a new

---

[43]George H. Sabine, *A History of Political Thought*, London: Harrap, 1963, p. 128.

[44]Ernst Troeltsch, *The Social Teaching of the Christian Churches and Groups*, O. Wyon, trans, New York: Harper Torchbooks, 1960, p. 64.

[45]*Ibid.*, p. 101.

order which (as the older and displaced order had laid claim to) purports to bring the "true truth." Such spirituality is itself an expression of the dissonance of the group whose beliefs threaten to dissemble and fade. The increased attention given to proselytizing at such times is one of the indicators of a belief system in jeopardy, and one of the inevitable responses to what Festinger has called cognitive dissonance.[46]

---

[46]Festinger's theory of cognitive dissonance attempts to describe the mechanisms behind the tendency of individuals to justify decisions that they have made. An individual whose investment has led to loss or failure will nonetheless justify the reasons for the investment in the first place or, on the other hand, he might find it necessary to justify his actions if they have in any manner infringed upon or disregarded the rules of his group. As Festinger explains, "Dissonance and consonance are relations among cognitions—that is, among opinions, beliefs, knowledge of the environment, and knowledge of one's own actions and feelings. Two opinions, or beliefs, or items of knowledge are *dissonant* with each other if they do not fit together—that is, if they are inconsistent, or if, considering only the particular two items, one does not follow from the other . . . Dissonance produces discomfort and, correspondingly, there will arise pressures to reduce or eliminate the dissonance. Attempts to reduce dissonance represent the observable manifestations that dissonance exists." Leon Festinger/Henry W. Riecken/Stanley Schachter, *When Prophecy Fails*, New York: Harper & Row Publishers, 1964, pp. 25, 26.

Festinger goes on to explain that there are three methods by which an individual may attempt to reduce dissonance. The first may be an attempt to "change one or more of the beliefs, opinions, or behaviors involved in the dissonance . . . ," the second "to acquire new information or beliefs that will increase the existing consonance and thus cause the total dissonance to be reduced," and the third "to forget or reduce the importance of those cognitions that are in a dissonant relationship." *Ibid.,* p. 26. One or all of these attempts may be employed. It is my contention that the transition from religious to psychological justifications we are presently undergoing is the result of an attempt to reduce the existing dissonance between religion and the empirical world view that presently predominates.

As Festinger has observed, "when people are committed to a belief and a course of action, clear disconfirming evidence may simply result in deepened conviction and increased proselyting." *Ibid.,* p. 12. This too is the position in which therapy presently finds itself.

vi.

The invagination of the horizon as a line of demarcation between the known and the unknown, between a visible upper and an invisible lower, the being-in-itself and the being-for-itself, is what would in time contribute to the creation of the idea of an unthought consciousness: an "unconscious" which is present but invisible and within which gyrates (according to the mechanistic analogies by which modern psychology defines the psyche) a machinery of powers as predictable and eternal in their movement as the stars of heaven. The doubling or folding of the horizon and the heavens gave birth to the idea of an "inside" more extensive than the phenomena delineating such a space allows. The libidinal "below" composed of energy and image, immediately inaccessible to the light of consciousness—first seeded in religion, watered by metaphysics, pruned by philosophy, and now plucked by psychology—is now defined as a dimension which "in its totality exceeds the limits of consciousness and therefore can never become the object of direct cognition."[47] This, along with the countless other statements of psychology regarding the nature of the unconscious, could have just as easily been stated by an Egyptian priest six thousand years ago in defining the other side of the horizon. Psychology now operates within this fold of our sensibilities, this primordial mirroring of the assigned Outer in an assigned inner. Phenomenal experience has been creased to the point where the identity of the psyche and the phenomenal world are oned.

Whereas the Egyptian left behind records indicating the degree to which the concept of interiority came into being through a folding of geographical reality to create the topological "inner" dimension, beginning the definition of the body's fold, the Greeks have left us indications of their concern with the creation of relation to a self. In the Egyptian experience, what we discover is that the psyche defines the felt experience of the overlap between body and world with the aid of a spatial linguistic—a language origi-

---

[47]C. G. Jung, *The Collected Works of*, (Hereafter, *CW*), New York: Pantheon Books, 1959, vol. 9ii, para. 40.

nally employed to derive meaning from the experience of natural phenomena.

The linguist A. J. Greimas has suggested that the differentiation of any original shapeless mass of experience may follow a "chronological order of production," hierarchical in structure.[48] Thus, in systematizing the semantics of space, spatiality is first differentiated into dimensionality and non-dimensionality, the former in turn differentiating into horizontality and verticality, the latter into surface and volume. The full series of differentiation is charted in the following manner[49]:

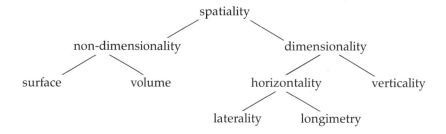

In either case—the transmission of the systematization of space from one culture to another, or the direct experience of such systematization by each culture because of a process of differentiation peculiar to the operations of the psyche (or even a combination of these two conditions)—it appears that cosmologies arise out of the psyche's interaction with natural phenomena.

It is apparent from my brief survey that the reality of the horizon and its peculiarities causes questions to be posed regarding one's existence—and that the most immediate have to do with questions regarding the nature of life and death which eventually give rise to metaphysics and eschatologies. When viewed from this perspective—one that would have been most apparent to the

---

[48]cf. Richard Harland's discussion of Griemas' principles of semantics in his *Superstructuralism: The Philosophy of Structuralism and Post-Structuralism*, London/New York: Methuen, 1987, p. 87.

[49]This illustration follows that given in Harland, *Superstructuralism*, p. 87.

Egyptian—the horizon gives birth to questions about which there are no definitive answers; the horizon defines a dimension that is both spiritual and divine *because* it represents what is inaccessible to the living. It was this folding that initially gave birth to ritual, religion, and mythology.

vii.

Moments before he died, Socrates reminded his friend that a cock should be offered to the God Asklepios, the standard contribution for having been cured of a disease. Such is the final legacy of the Socratic tradition—that life be perceived as an illness to be cured. Since that time the Socratic message has become mandatory and routine. The Egyptians first developed the story of what it is we must do with a forgotten and dead memory—what presently constitutes the Twentieth Century idea of a complex. In this sense therapy's precursor was the art of Egyptian mummification in that it too seeks to keep the "dead thing" alive, close to the chest, divinized and immortal. The repressed, the complex, (when "discovered") is excavated for its organs, the autonomous things that make it tick. We speak of the dead but animating memories as autonomous complexes as if they were gods, and by so doing *give* them the autonomy to display themselves as such. The patient's fear becomes personified by powers that—by the nature of their assigned divinity—he has no control over. At the most, he may learn to relate to them by a thorough religious conversion almost hallucinatory in nature—one in which courage is not to be found in the profundity of a personal decision to act as a statement of *becoming*, but in the luxuriant excuse that something other than himself did the prompting: Aphrodite, or Pan, or some other god or goddess that has given one license to be, and that may ultimately be pointed to as the cause of anything that might go wrong in such personal decisions. There, in the realm of images, we are told true life, psychic life, begins.

But no one has really asked, What if these are *not* Gods and Goddesses? What if this tempestuous demand for and flood of images is the personification of some other order? What if the images are merely the transitory personifications of structures perpetually in need of updating and revision? What if revision is simply the attempt of the individual to be maintained in the *status quo* condition of a continuously shifting concept of normality? What if therapy as it is now practiced is actually a technique whereby the individual is adjusted, corrected, and maneuvered into a model of the self which is symptomatic of society's own woundedness—if the manner in which the dialectic encounter is conducted does not simply keep that wound open?

Such in fact is the therapy that has come into being, a technique developed to create a psychic symmetry patterned after natural phenomena. The movement of the circumpolar stars in ancient Greece after which the psyche should be modeled is now turned into the idea of a natural psyche damaged by the vicissitudes of being. The fold that turned upper into inner has also led to an explanation of individual differences as being but the products of a derangement of the circuits of the self in each individual person. Here too is the source of the technique to correct those differences. We are witness to the development of Plato's story and the transformation of power on its way to becoming its own truth.

It was during Plato's time that the power of religion, which sought to keep its wisdom for the few, began to be displaced by a philosophy that sought to make of wisdom a public truth through the power of public law. But power is immanent and dispersed throughout the whole of society. It is neither owned by virtue of social position nor won by achievement:

> "What makes power hold good, what makes it accepted, is simply the fact that it doesn't only weigh on us as a force that says no, but that it traverses and produces things, it induces pleasure, forms of knowledge, produces discourse. It needs to be considered as a productive network which runs through the whole social body, much more than as a negative instance whose function is repression."[50]

Power is not to be misconstrued as the imposition of rules. In Foucault's thought rules arise out of the conditions within which social action occur. That is, rules are not socially imposed but are instead generated out of practices. He also emphasizes that these

---

[50]Foucault, *Power/Knowledge*, p. 119.

practices are neither arbitrary nor accidental—they are regulated by the reciprocal relations existing between power and knowledge.

What makes power also hold true to its intent is the elegance of the story it creates. Plato's story stays with us in the practice of therapy—as do the concept of the ideal person, the technique that creates such a person, and the storied structures of the psyche. The technique Plato proposed has led to a form of person-engineering that brings about the creation of a false identity. It is a form of power that

> ". . . applies itself to immediate everyday life which categorizes the individual, marks him by his own individuality, attaches him to his own identity, imposes a law of truth on him which he must recognize and which others have to recognize in him. It is a form of power which makes individuals subjects. There are two meanings of the word subject: subject to someone else by control and dependence, and tied to his own identity by a conscience or self-knowledge. Both meanings suggest a form of power which subjugates and makes subject to."[51]

viii.

The fiction of psychology is that of a nonexistent and mythologized inside, a Platonic cosmogony resting upon the shoulders of the Cartesian proposition that mind is of another order than body, following other rules and rulerships. But what if we allow that there is no given interior—that our experience of interiority occurs because of our relationship with the world—that the nature of the person is determined at that juncture where the world is folded? Merleau-Ponty suggests this when he proposes that the experience of the lived body is another "genus of being,"[52] a third mode of being that resolves the Cartesian split:

> "[It] is neither that of being in itself nor that of being for itself but, as it were, the dialectical synthesis of the two. As perceptual

---

[51]Foucault in Hubert L. Dreyfus, Paul Rabinow, *Michel Foucault: Beyond Structuralism and Hermeneutics*, Chicago: The University of Chicago Press, 1983, p. 212.

[52]M. Merleau-Ponty, *Phenomenology of Perception*, Colin Smith, trans., London: Routledge & Kegan Paul, 1967, p. 350.

consciousness I am not a pure subject, I am not a consciousness *of* my body; I *am* this massive and opaque body which *knows itself.*"[53]

What this means is that the two Cartesian orders of the physical and the mental meet, that subject and object, interior and exterior overlap, that one is no more in or out of the other than the other. We then have no true "interior" as a given, but rather a process created by the interaction of the world and a myself.

The ancients believed the horizon contained beyond it another realm, another space containing what would in time become the Euclidian laws of the phenomenal world; so too does the idea of the unconscious assume a demarcated area where unused life in the form of memory is contained, becomes lost, dies and is reborn, becoming "the receptacle of all lost memories."[54] The concept of the unconscious as container is based upon the same supposition that a Cartesian consciousness is based upon—that consciousness is a clearly defined space given with being; that consciousness exists as a space into which information and experience are deposited and stored. But if consciousness is neither a space nor dimension but a process, then we are forced to revise what the unconscious also might be. If it were no more a space than consciousness, but likewise a process, then one would be faced with the immediate difficulty of explaining how we can treat the unconscious as a given and subjective psychic *dimension*. This idea of the unconscious, specifically the collective unconscious, as a process, was a position that Jung held but which has been essentially ignored in contemporary Jungian thought.[55] I would now go even further to propose that the unconscious is not even a process, but is instead an ephemeral property of consciousness at its presumed terminus—the product of a series of foldings, neither a given and structured domain, nor a process of anything other than consciousness.

---

[53]Gary Brent Madison, *The Phenomenology of Merleau-Ponty*, Athens, Ohio: Ohio University Press, 1981, p. 39.

[54]Jung, *CW*, vol. 8., para. 270.

[55]"Only after I had familiarized myself with alchemy did I realize that the unconscious is a process. C. G. Jung, *Memories, Dreams, Reflections*, New York: Vintage Books, 1965, p. 209. Jung's italics.

ix.

Fuerbach had originally proposed that religion is created by a "projective spirit." In other words, that it is the nature of the human psyche to project an *a priori* structure onto the world:

> "And here it may be applied, without any limitation, the proposition: the object of any subject is nothing else than the subject's own nature taken objectively. Such as are a man's thoughts and dispositions, such is his God . . . Consciousness of God is self-consciousness, knowledge of God is self-knowledge. . . . God is the manifested inward nature, the expressed self of a man . . . the being of man is alone the real being of God—man is the real God. And if in the consciousness which man has of God first arises the self-consciousness of God, then the human consciousness is *per se*, the divine consciousness. Why then dost thou alienate man's consciousness from him, and make it the self-consciousness of a being distinct from man, of that which is an object to him?"[56]

Admittedly, this was a bold and original perception, one that sought to return the self to its own operational ground. Even though Feuerbach's proposal was based upon the misapprehension of the topology created by the fold as an *a priori*, he nonetheless revealed the inevitability of such unfoldings—projection. Freud pushed Feuerbach's idea further when he postulated the existence of an organizing and controlling structure—the superego—as being but the internalization of composited social directives. His was one of the first clear proposals that individuals not only "internalize" social reality, but that the social factors so internalized assume an autonomous existence, acting as if they had always been innate components of the psyche. Whereas Feuerbach had discovered the principles of psychological "projection," establishing it as the machinery by which the psyche casts itself into and across the plane of phenomenal reality, Freud intimated (in part) that at least one psychic structure was the result of an internalization of the social world. What he alluded to as an internalization was actually the experience of the fold of psychological

---

[56]Ludwig Feuerbach, *The Essence of Christianity*, George Eliot, trans., New York: Harper Torchbooks, 1957, pp. 12-13, 230.

truths, a new cosmogony that proposed ultimately to identify the source of good and evil within the person.

These original insights should have alerted us to the degree that the psyche not only becomes structured by its interaction with the world, but then polices itself along the lines of external mores. It is in this sense that stricture and structure become synonymous. From this we should have learned that it is the nature of the psyche to objectify its experiences of the phenomenal world by acquisitioning and defining them as proof of its own composition and structure. That is to say, the psyche defines and gives boundaries to itself via what it understands as an "internalization" of collectively approved values, and by so doing legitimates itself as an integral aspect of the world or of society. All human behavior, inasmuch as it occurs in the foreground of social reality, arises out of and is in response to systems of value. Every member of a group believes that such values are but the inevitable result of critical evaluations regarding phenomenal experience. Rarely are values questioned unless they interrupt the economy of facilitated gestures—the language of a group that allows immediate comprehension and response.

We fail to see that the values which initially organize the psyche, while indeed in each period having contemporary validity, are stories. They represent the machinery of society's organization, and to that extent simply reflect what society needs the psyche to be at that particular point in history. In other words, what we think of the psyche determines not only its very structure, but the manner in which it thinks of and perceives reality. Rarely do we appreciate that it is by this natural and inherent process of "psyche" that we invent metaphysical and psychological systems which do nothing more than justify the assumption that consciousness and mind are *a priori* structures that give shape to the world.

Let us here assume that the structure of the psyche is the result of a process which first delineates its ephemerality by the mirroring of phenomena, and then achieves a semblance of structure by the repetition of its interpretation of those phenomena personified. It is then possible that a similar process leads to the creation of the idea of the unconscious. We have already seen how the folding of geographical and astronomical realities leads to an experience of a subjective internalization that eventually gives rise to the topology of an unconscious, of how the inevitable assumptions regarding natural phenomena became institutionalized "facts," doctrinal truths that have now surfaced in the science of psychology as it seeks to create the definitive image of the person. From this, it was seen how in all likelihood the ontological questions that gave rise to eschatological religions had their origins in this event as well. What all of this suggests is that the unconscious is neither a location nor a container, but merely an aspect of consciousness the dynamics of which are concealed and denied by our identifying it as the parameters of another order of being—and that the concept of the unconscious simply illustrates the operation of an archetype.[57]

When Jung defined the collective unconscious as the "repository of man's experience," and an "image of the world which has taken aeons to form,"[58] he also inadvertently allowed that the collective unconscious is an archetype. In other words, that the collective unconscious is a "primordial image," which is

> "always collective (elsewhere also termed the 'archetype') a mnemic deposit, an *imprint* . . . which has arisen through a condensation of innumerable, similar processes . . . a typical base form of a certain ever-recurring psychic experience . . . The primordial image is the preliminary stage of the idea [archetype] . . . its maternal soil."[59]

But let us press further, for he also informs us that by the term "idea" he means

> "something which expresses the meaning of a primordial image that has been abstracted or detached from the concretism of the image . . . hence it is a transcendent concept which, as such, transcends the limit of experiencable things."[60]

---

[57]I had in an earlier work begun the redefinition of the archetype by showing it to be the personified amalgamation of culturally embedded ideas that then coalesce into an Institution. cf. my, "On the Possession of Consciousness," in *Working the Soul: Reflections on Jungian Psychology*, Berkeley: North Atlantic Books, 1988, pp. 152ff.

[58]Jung, *CW*, vol 7, para. 151. My emphasis. Also see *Ibid.*, para. 507.

[59]C. G. Jung, *Psychological Types*, H. Godwyn Baynes trans., New York: Harcourt, Brace & Company, Inc., 1923, pp. 555ff. Jung's italics.

[60]*Ibid.*, p. 548.

What we are being told is that the "idea" or image of the collective unconscious has been formed by human history over the passage of aeons. However, Jung located the idea beyond the limit of human history by claiming it as "an a priori existing and determining psychological factor,"[61] adding that it "in its totality exceeds the limits of consciousness and therefore can never become the object of direct cognition,"[62] transcending what can be experienced. The word "transcendence" has its root in the Latin *transcendere*, "to raise oneself beyond." Kant, whom Jung cites while defining the archetype as transcendent, informs us that the transcendent is what is beyond possible experience. But Husserl brings us to a sharper consideration when he stated that

> "The pure thing seen, what is visible 'of' the thing, is first of all
> a surface, and in the changing course of seeing I see it now from
> this 'side,' now from that, continuously perceiving it from ever
> differing sides. But in them *the* surface exhibits itself to me in a
> continuous synthesis; each side is for consciousness a manner of
> exhibition *of* it. This implies that, while the surface is
> immediately given, I mean more than it offers . . . In seeing I
> always 'mean' it with all the sides which are in no way given to
> me . . . Thus every perception has 'for consciousness,' a *horizon*
> belonging to its object (i.e., whatever is meant in the percep-
> tion).[63]

Presented with a cube, I am only present to one side of it, but none-the-less intend its completeness—I "see" it as a cube. But the fact remains that I can never actually see the cube in its totality. Presented at every instance with but one side, my intentionality transcends the actual event. I "see" what is not perceptually visible to me, what my eyes cannot perceive. I perceive what is not possible within the limits of human experience: I transcend the one-sided presentation of the cube in order to perceive the entire cube at once. Whenever we "raise ourselves beyond" what is actually

---

[61]*Ibid.*, p. 548.

[62]Jung, *CW*, vol. 9ii, para. 40.

[63]Edmund Husserl, *The Crisis of European Sciences and Transcendental Phenomenology*, David Carr, trans., Evanston: Northwestern University Press, 1970, pp. 157-8.

given, we therefore transcend the object and experience transcendence. We can therefore agree that

> "What makes any object 'transcendent,' having genuine otherness, is locatable in this play of presence and absence-in-presence in our perception of things. But note that transcendence is constituted *within* experience, experience carefully analyzed."[64]

It is this intending characteristic of consciousness that when folded gives rise to the idea of the *a priori* as a philosophical and religious principle. It is what gives certainty to the idea of an ontological other-side to the horizon, and what would in time give birth to the idea of both a personal and collective unconscious. The collective unconscious, therefore, is the image of the historicity of the invaginating process by which consciousness comprehends the substantiality and consistency of the world as a pre-existent object—as that which exists before the individual. It is the latency of our presence in the world. But the idea of the collective unconscious cannot come into being, cannot become a latency, unless it is folded into subjectivity.

Jung has taken this doubling of the transcendence of the phenomenal world and inverted it to posit the existence of a transcendent principle existing at the base of the human psyche—the collective unconscious. That is, Jung correctly saw the degree to which imbedded historical institutions compose the dimension of intersubjectivity.[65] He mistook, however, the folding of this imbeddedness for a characteristic of the human organism, claiming that the collective unconscious

> ". . . is not an individual acquisition but is rather the functioning of the inherited brain structure, which in its broad outlines is the same in all human beings . . . The inherited brain is the product of our ancestral life. It consists of the structural deposits of equiv-

---

[64]Don Ihde, *Experimental Phenomenology*, New York: G. P. Putnam's Sons, 1977, p. 63.

[65]"It seems to me that their [the archetypes] origin can only be explained by assuming them to be deposits of the constantly repeated experiences of humanity." Jung, *CW*, vol. 7, para. 109.

alents of psychic activities which were repeated innumerable times in the life of our ancestors."[66]

It is in this primordial image of the world, the *archetype* called the collective unconscious, where, Jung informs us, other archetypes *per se* are located, where they have crystallized to become "the ruling power, the gods, images of the dominant law and principles, and of typical regularly occurring events in the soul's cycle of experience."[67] (Or what appear to be typically recurring events but are more than likely the redressing of existing values so that they might incorporate necessary additions or revisions.) Because the archetypes are the "effect and deposit of experience that have already taken place, [actually appearing] as the factors which cause such experiences,"[68] they answer the descriptions of institutions—such institutions as marriage, friendship, war, etc.

Furthermore, an archetype is defined by Jung as being the self-portrait of an instinct, "the *instinct's perception of itself.*"[69] About these instincts, he writes:

"Instincts are typical modes of action, and wherever we meet with uniform and regularly recurring modes of action and reaction we are dealing with instinct, no matter whether it is associated with a conscious motive or not."[70]

But as William James has stressed, the instincts conform to a general reflex type and are in essence impulses which, in an animal with memory, cease to be blind and impulsive once the instinctive act has been repeated.[71] Thus, instinctive acts are modified through their encounter with life circumstances and give rise to

---

[66]Jung, *CW*, vol. 17, para. 207.

[67]Jung, *CW*, vol 7, para. 151. Also see CW, vol. 18, para. 1536 where Jung simply states that the collective unconscious is the totality of the archetypes.

[68]Jung, *CW*, vol 7, para. 151, footnote #3.

[69]Jung, *CW*, vol. 8 para. 277. Jung's italics.

[70]*Ibid.*, para. 273. Jung's italics.

[71]William James, *The Principles of Psychology*, New York: Dover Publications, 1950, Vol. Two, pp. 384, 385, 390.

decisions to be made regarding the apparent choices the environment offers:

> "This leads us to the *law of transitoriness*, which is this: *Many instincts ripen at a certain age and then fade away.* A consequence of this law is that if, during the time of such an instinct's vivacity, objects adequate to arouse it are met with, a *habit* of acting on them is formed, which remains when the original instinct has passed away; but that if no such objects are met with, then no habit will be formed; and, later on in life, when the animal meets the objects, he will altogether fail to react, as at the earlier epoch he would instinctively have done . . . The natural conclusion to draw from this transciency of instincts is that *most instincts are implanted for the sake of giving rise to habits, and that, this purpose once accomplished, the instincts themselves, as such, have no raison d'etre in the psychical economy, and consequently fade away.*"[72]

A considerable degree of credibility must be given to James' law of transitoriness in that few of us react out of a base of raw and blind instinctuality. It is inevitable that anyone living in a society or community will be subjected to the socialization techniques whose purpose it is to modify and alter (if not repress) instinctual nature. That being the case, the archetypes cannot be spoken of as but the images of the instincts. Instead, they must be seen as a result of the habituated modifications a society has brought to bear upon the instincts. They are socially designed habits whose staying powers are far more tenacious than those of the instincts. These archetypes, or social habits, constitute a society's stock of knowledge which are irrevocably imposed on individuals through a socialization technique, which in the final analysis is a coding procedure. The specificity of any archetypal role is governed by the differentiation of general knowledge "according to which knowledge is (or is considered to be) relevant for certain typical problems and for certain typical persons."[73]

---

[72]*Ibid.*, Vol. Two, pp. 398, 402. James' italics. James adds that it is obvious that some instincts are not as transient as others, stating that the instincts of self-preservation and feeding may not be transient at all. However, suicide and anorexia nervosa seem to indicate that even these instincts may express transciency.

[73]Alfred Schutz & Thomas Luckman, *The Structure of the Life-World,* Evanston, Ill: Northwestern University Press, 1973, p. 291.

The application of specific forms of knowledge—the special-
ized "solutions" to the recurring inevitabilities of human biology
(i.e., the province of medicine) or social organization (i.e., laws,
distribution of rights, roles, etc.)—become imbedded in Institutions which are maintained from generation to generation.
Everyone has access to these solutions through individuals who
have been initiated, schooled or otherwise prepared to perform
within the parameters of these knowledge-roles. It is out of such
a dynamic that we acquire what are referred to as the archetypal
roles of Doctor, Nurse, Soldier, Nurse, Mother, Father, etc. In
other words, the "archetypes," are indeed "of" a collective unconscious, but the collective unconscious is a culturally produced *perspective* of a society's world-view concerning the origin and nature
of the values its predecessors held. It is, as Jung said, an image
of the past that explains the present. Only by failing to see the
degree to which such social institutions, along with the rules,
roles, and laws that constitute them are socially determined, are
we then prompted to seek their origin in the darkness of prehistory,
inevitably finding satisfaction in the story of a transmundane source.

This experience of transmundality is but a concomitant portion
of the Husserlian "natural attitude" towards everyday life—the
pre-reflective enmeshment in one's naive acceptance of the world
as it is presented. This natural attitude is synonymous with Jung's
collective unconscious which "does not . . . owe its existence to
personal experience and consequently is not a personal acquisition."[74] Interiority is not its domain: it is a value-laden perception
that intercepts and indiscriminately spreads itself over the out-
flowing stream of our consciousness long prior to the possibility
of our recognizing that one does not truly see with one's eyes
". . . things exterior to myself who sees them: [but instead realizes
that] they are exterior only to my body, not to my thought, which
soars over it as well as them."[75]

The idea of a collective unconscious as a genetically inherited
dimension is a hindrance to and not an ally of all investigations

---

[74]Jung, *CW*, vol. 9i, para. 88.

[75]Maurice Merleau-Ponty, *The Visible and the Invisible*, Evanston, Ill:
Northwestern University Press, 1968, p. 30.

into the nature of consciousness. The proposal that the collective unconscious is an internal and integrated structure predicating what the nature of being should be even before being *is*, is against the explorative possibilities of the type of an awareness peculiar to human beings.

Jung states that this "historical mirror-image of the world . . . is a world, but a world of images."[76] The images are obviously the archetypes, which he also tells us are perspectives, ways of seeing:

> *"Archetypes are typical modes of apprehension, and wherever we meet with uniform and regularly recurring modes of apprehension we are dealing with an archetype, no matter whether its mythological character is recognized or not."*[77]

I had earlier mentioned that power on the way to becoming truth becomes personified in story. The "modes of apprehension" Jung states the archetypes are, are the legitimating stories of truth. Each archetype, or institutional role, always presents itself as the true personification of the function it intends. These stories of truth are fulfilled within the dimension of the natural attitude by persons in society to the degree that they identify, or agree, with the roles or the truth assigned to those roles. It is in this manner that individuals become the personification of the archetypes.

The proposition that the archetypes are eternal and *a priori*, also tacitly assumes that they are therefore supreme values—predetermined ways or possibilities of being. Such beliefs bring to becoming an order and structure foreign to it. "Becoming" is disorder until it discovers being through meaning. The force that "becoming" is eventually seeks to become Truth through the imposition of meaning. Meaning is the ground within and upon which a truth is constructed, a site specific to a determination. Therefore, what an archetype represents is the "truth" of an imposed value. It is the image of a specific type of power. The archetypes represent the socially defined limits of experiential behavior.

The individual is as much enmeshed and penetrated by the story as he is by either power or knowledge. In fact, the legitimiza-

---

[76]Jung, *CW*, vol. 7, para. 507.
[77]Jung, *CW*, vol. 8, para. 280. Jung's italics.

tion of the story, its viability for transformation into the truth depends upon the degree to which it can convincingly entrance. I have in an earlier work indicated that the truth and power structures which comprise the natural attitude give rise to two specific programs most commonly employed to define primitive modes of societal interaction—trance and non-trance possession techniques designed to promote specific types of social communication.[78] If the collective unconscious is anything, it is a society's grammar from which a language of its social fictions is constructed, all of which are concealed in the bright glare of the natural attitude. It is at this dark altar where therapy presently kneels.

The greatest difficulty with the present notion of the collective unconscious is with its depiction as an original unity. The concept of the collective unconscious presupposes that the diversity of phenomena is the expression of an orderliness against which chance occurrences simply refer us to a hidden and concealed meaning, an order, if one only had eyes and ears to see and hear it. Thus, even the acausal connecting principle of synchronicity that Jung proposed suggests nothing more than that chance is meaningful if it is properly read. That is, all chance can be subsumed under the canopy of an original and morally superior unity. All of which is to say that there is no chance, only misunderstood circumstance.

A psyche located in a world without chance becomes bound by meaning, troubled by the accident that cannot be signed by meaning, the illness or disease that will not simply reflect back an absence of moral or ethical failure. What this inevitably gives birth to is a therapy that denies differences (finding in them resistances) in favor of a uniformity of experience that belies the undifferentiated multiplicity necessary for any truly creative expression. The person emerging from such a therapeutic encounter sacrifices the inherent potential of a consciousness that reaches far beyond itself for the restrictive and fallacious idea of a wholeness that actually serves nothing more than a social imperative. Such wholeness— itself but the imputation of geometric and mathematical attempts to establish a divinely sanctioned *nomos* in the figure of the circle

---

[78]Ponce, *Working*, pp. 156ff.

and its center[79]—limits becoming, as well as the being that it becomes. Where synchronicity abounds in a personal life there we can expect to find a fear of diversity, change, and chance occurrence.

Nor should this call for the continuing genesis of diversity and multiplicity be mistaken for a polytheism of either ancient or modern classification. Polytheism ultimately demands that consciousness be subservient to a pantheon of powers, each demanding its own altar. Polytheism is but a method by which the potential diversity of the psyche is seemingly allowed its expression, while at the same time defining chance expressions as *foci* around which the psyche must nonetheless organize itself. Each god or power, i.e., each chance quality, becomes defined and limited by personification and story. Every deity can become a center, the ritual obeisance offered it the lineaments of the fiction of its wholeness. True, one may honor first this deity and then that deity—but chance and diversity so approached dishonors the meaning of their expression and imposes upon the psyche a rule of order that is not of its making.

X.

The concept of the archetype, of an *a priori*, which is genetically *of* our bodies rather than inscribed on our bodies, diverts us from the problems created by the play of consciousness. We interpret the difficulties of both our personal and social natures as failures to meet transcendent demands and values. In other words, we are diverted from the interplay, the activity that actually occurs in the in-between space we as social actors not only occupy but define and fill through the agency and language of consciousness, in both its linguistic and non-linguistic expressions.

When a body-politic ascribes to its own power divine attributes, it relieves each individual within its reach of all personal

---

[79]*vide*, "The transcendent function does not proceed without aim and purpose, but leads to the revelation of the essential man . . . The symbols used by the unconscious to this end are the same as those which mankind has always used to express wholeness, completeness, and perfection . . . the quaternity and the circle." Jung, *CW*, vol. 7, para. 186.

and individual responsibilities. All personal failures may then be attributed to an inability to understand or meet eternally established *a prioris*, archetypes, which are not under the control of consciousness.[80] If we wish to have consciousness effected (i.e., corrected or normalized) by these archetypes, we are again told, we must establish a relationship with them that is *in agreement* with the values they represent.[81] From this we can see that values define behavior through constraint and restraint and must therefore also be understood as forces. It is at such a juncture that pathology is born: pathology is the result of an individual's *agreement with values given as fixed and immutable* but which are in fact experienced (for whatever reason) as unattainable, existing beyond the range of one's capabilities—capabilities too often described (and thereby limited by such description) in terms of a coding system that distributes rights along the agreement lines of graphs grading occupational, racial, religious, monetary, and political worth. Pathology occurs because of a differentiation of desire. The terms of the differentiation are in accord with values that design human liberties, these latter assigned to gradated levels of societally determined levels of power and rights. Pathology is the cement of a consensus reality—it is the stuff that shores the beach of the natural attitude's occupation of a "reality," content in its walled containment, certain of its establishment and longevity. Pathology is desire diverted.

xi.

Aristotle reminds us that whereas the earliest gods also represented general states, Eros had from its religious beginnings been presented as a principle which "will move things and bring them together."[82] In other words, the motion of the universe is

---

[80]Jung, *CW*, vol. 5, paras. 467, 617.

[81]*Ibid.*, para 450. Jung's comments regarding ritual as a mode by which the unconscious and its archetypes may be purposefully activated is an example of such agreement.

[82]Jonathan Barnes, editor, *The Complete Works of Aristotle*, Princeton: Princeton University Press, 1984, Vol. II, *Metaphysics* 984b, 24-31. All references to Aristotle will be to this edition unless otherwise indicated.

desire, encompassed in a philosophical principle when Empedocles assigned the status of prime mover to the goddess Aphrodite.[83] In another sense, the true beginning of the Western concept of desire rests somewhere concomitant to Socrates' proposal that it arose from want or lack:

> "And therefore, whoever feels a want is wanting something which is not yet to hand, and the object of his love and of his desire is whatever he isn't; or whatever he hasn't got—that is to say, whatever he is lacking in."[84]

This discourse establishes that the object of this "want and lack of" is the immortal and beautiful which may be achieved only through a process of weaning first from the love of bodies, then from the love of institutions and learning, until one finally has "universal beauty . . . [dawn] upon his inward sight."[85] Plato refines these moves, emphasizing the necessary sublimation of sexual desire and activity so that one may successfully leave behind the field of Aphrodite Pandemus "whose nature partakes of both male and female," and enter into the immediacy and worship of Aphrodite Urania, "whose attributes have nothing of the female, but are altogether male . . . and innocent of any hint of lewdness."[86] The program of therapy suggested by the Socratic/Platonic tradition is therefore that of a sublimation of mortal desire in favor of immortal desire. Pathology, as understood today, is the embodiment of the Socratic definition modernized: one's pathology is implicitly defined as a result of the lack of the whole and the beautiful, the image of which is that of a cosmic mind damaged by its becoming as being.

When Freud reiterates that the function of Eros (now personified as the god Eros) "is to establish ever greater unities and to preserve them thus—in short, to bind together,"[87] desire once

---

[83]Kathleen Freeman, trans., *Ancilla to the Pre-Socratic Philosophers*, Cambridge: Harvard University Press, 1971, p. 53.

[84]*Symposium*, 200f.

[85]*Symposium*, 211b.

[86]*Symposium*, 180d, 181b,c.

[87]Sigmund Freud, "The Theory of the Instincts," in *An Outline of Psychoanalysis*, Clara Thompson, editor, New York: Modern Library, 1955, p. 6.

again fully enters the world-stage as *the* vehicle of transformation. In the same passage Freud reveals that the term "libido" is but a synonym for Eros who as a force in the human body regresses to earlier stages in human development to cause psychic illness. The goal of psychoanalysis, as of Platonic discourse before it, is to free the regressed and repressed life force so that the complete individual might be realized. With the Twentieth-Century introduction of Eros as *the* principle power of the human psyche, a new chapter in mythology began. Contrary to what he thought he was accomplishing, Freud did not serve a death blow to religion—he relocated it deep within us, turning the human body into a new Olympus and tragedian's stage.

The psychoanalytic differentiation of desire/libido generated a discourse (or story) that established its truth in the technique of psychoanalysis. The "truth" of this technique (buoyed by its subservience to a medical model of health) in turn justified the directing and socialization of the concept "desire" to fit the newly created modern world. Implicit in such a perspective was the concept of an ideal person, along with the necessity of a program or programs of person-management that would guarantee the production of a medically approved norm. All subjective desire was to be understood as the manifestation of an underlying and parent Desire—a desire which was but the expression of the "natural," itself imbued with the inherent ethicality of Nature that could only be accessed through the enlightened application of reason. Desire, or Eros, had to be discovered before it could be truly experienced.

Whatever Eros was to ancient Greece—whether the basis of an aesthetic, an explanation of sexuality or love, or a vehicle for transformation—it has now been engineered to limit the expression of the measure of being. As T.S. Eliot put it, we have been taught to measure out our life in coffee spoons. Desire has fully progressed into a need for what we have been told it is that we lack—and what we lack, unless we have been appropriately processed (we are assured), is the type of psychological wholeness the definition of which not only shifts from one psychological school to another, but from one state, hospital, or governmental agency to another. If one finds oneself with a desire, then he is to be shown that its latent cause is the beauty and truth of the unknown, the forgotten, the soon-to-be-found-out. The definition

45

will be discovered in a symptomatology of desire compiled to define what it is that you don't have, and who you are that you are not. And behind every such definition is to be found a general premise regarding the structure and dynamic operations of the psyche, practically all of which presume the existence of an unconscious.

xii.

As Edward Sapir, along with others, stressed in the first half of this century:

> "Human beings do not live in the objective world alone, nor alone in the world of social activity as ordinarily understood, but are very much at the mercy of the particular language which has become the medium of expression for their society . . . No two languages are ever sufficiently similar to be considered as representing the same social reality. The world in which different societies live are distinct worlds, not merely the same world with different labels attached . . . We see and hear and otherwise experience very largely as we do because the language habits of our community predispose certain choices of interpretation."[88]

In other words, each culture interprets, assigns meaning to, and constructs the world in a manner different from any another culture. In the final analysis no one culture holds the key to unlocking a truly objective world view, but each creates a language by which a "reality" can be consistently presented to and represented by each of its members. Each culture wears its own signature, an ephemeral body germinated out of codes its members must learn and embody so that the collective image of the world might be first apprehended and then comprehended. This signature, for the reasons offered, can never be described as a universal *a priori*, but only as the sign of a particular group's consensus of reality—a social *a priori*.

Saussure also alerted us to the fact that language is a system of signs that express ideas; each culture is constructed of signs that attend to and bring attention to either an aspect of reality, or a com-

---

[88]Edward Sapir, *Selected Writings in Language Culture and Personality*, David G. Mandelbaum, editor, Berkeley: University of California Press, 1949, p. 162.

plete reality—and those signs are also expressed through non-linguistic languages.[89] In other words, every reality is coded and expresses itself through a language. If, as Saussure states, anthropological facts, customs, and rituals fall within the realm of semiotics, the study of signs,[90] and if the unconscious refers us to a coding activity of language, then one would expect to become capable of discerning the effect of this activity within the realm of social objects. The facts that we are given about the world or of reality are actually signs, images, or stories about facts.

It is in its desire to locate and situate itself that the psyche codes its experience. Its creation of multiple realities within one cultural setting is its play; the permutations it creates are expressions of its desire to spread itself across the full ground of becoming. It is a willingness or need to become embodied, to stay rooted in what sustains it. The psyche personifies the sovereignty of its own power in the images that are the signs of its own knowledge. The fictionalization of its power is what has been left us in mythologies. The gods inhabiting these mythologies are the discarded permutations of the psyche's legitimations of itself during an historical period when their personifications were truths. What we discover in mythology is the clustering of societal relations *as they had existed in another time and in another culture*—as well as the manner in which they had originally been distributed throughout the social body.

xiii.

If language defines reality and exists before the individual, then the learning of a language is the learning of a specific type of reality. In addition, if in order to think we must first have language, then in effect we must be taught a reality in order to think. From this it follows that we cannot experience subjectivity without language—for what is experienced in the "experience" of subjec-

---

[89]Ferdinand de Saussure, *Course in General Linguistics*, Wade Baskin, trans., Charles Bally, Albert Sechehaye, & Albert Riedlinger, editors, New York: McGraw-Hill Book Company, 1966, pp. 15-17.

[90]*Ibid.*, p. 15.

tivity is a "myself" *thinking* about subjectivity. I cannot think about myself without a language. But language exists indiscriminately throughout society,[91] the property of no one person, dependent upon a community of speakers—never existing "apart from the social fact . . . [because] its social nature is one of its inner characteristics."[92] To employ language a person must first have access to the social world which gives him language—and it is through and of this social world that he thinks, for his thinking is of things, objects, ideas, and other actors which would not exist if it were not because of this social world.

The object of thinking is the acquisition of meaning, and the locale of its activity is always described as "inner," this concept in turn always presumed to be accompanied by the ancillary aspect of "depth." The employment of these terms to describe the phenomenon of thinking does more than intimate that it occurs within a circumscribed inner space; it also forces us to assume that the unconscious is similarly delineated. In addition, it is also presumed that it is within this latter dimension that language is stored. But such assumptions are antiquated insofar as it now understood that language "is a function of differentiation and signification . . . [a] network of differences [that] cannot be localized in the brain or anywhere else," and that "it is a social function overdetermined by the complex process of exchange and social tasks, produced by it, and incomprehensible without it."[93]

That the location of language is not the human body but the social world can only mean thinking is an activity performed *in* the world. In other words, our thinking occurs "outside" of us, in language as it has been folded over. Clearly, it is from a semantics of space that we have appropriated the terms "interior" and "depth" to describe and locate the operation of language, the process of thinking, and the origin of meaning, the latter arising out of the decipherment of activity given and received on the surface of events.

---

[91]*Ibid.*, p. 73.

[92]*Ibid.*, p. 77.

[93]Julia Kristeva, *Language: The Unknown*, New York: Columbia University Press, 1989, pp. 19-20.

The depth that we ascribe to meaning, which inevitably arises out of a reflection of past events, is achieved through a comparison of differences between the effects that different events have given rise to in the past. In reflection, it is the past event that we measure, and by so doing remain with the event as having passed. The meaning I discover in any given situation is simply the way I have been taught to organize the past, from which all meaning derives—for meaning can never be located in an event as it is occurring, only after it has occurred.[94] By recognizing that lived experiences initially exist without definition in the stream of consciousness, that they have been lived but not structured and valenced, Alfred Schutz has pointed out (as Bergson before him) that a past experience only acquires meaning when it has been isolated and lifted out of the stream. This definition of the past is accomplished through the act of reflection "which belongs in the spatiotemporal world of everyday life."[95] However, we need not isolate and lift experiences "out" of something to assign them meaning. Deleuze's commentary on Bergson reveals that because of the contemporaneity of the past and the present they

> ". . . do not denote two successive moments, but two elements which coexist: One is the present, which does not cease to pass, and the other is the past, which does not cease to be but through which all presents pass. It is in this sense that there is a pure past, a kind of 'past in general'. The past does not follow the present, but on the contrary, is presupposed by it as the pure condi-

---

[94]"Because the concept of meaningful experience always presupposes that the experience of which meaning is predicated is a discrete one, it now becomes quite clear that only a past experience can be called meaningful, that is, one that is present to the retrospective glance as already finished and done with . . . Only the already experienced is meaningful, not that which is being experienced." Alfred Schutz, *The Phenomenology of the Social World*, Evanston, Ill.: Northwestern University Press, 1967, p. 52.

[95]ibid., p. 45. These proposals lie at the heart of the exploratory inquires of this book, for recollection is the vehicle which carries almost all of the therapeutic process. That even the act of recollection becomes socially structured is of crucial significance if we are to understand what therapy is, or could be.

tion which it would not pass. In other words, each present goes back to itself as past . . . The past is 'contemporaneous' with the present that it has been.[96]

But where, one may justly ask, is the past *contained*, where does memory exist if not *in* the unconscious?

Plato had proposed that knowledge is actually the result of *anamesis*, or the recollection of what we had known in a prenatal state.[97] It is by this process that the *eide* ("ideas" or what we presently refer to as the archetypes) may be known. The argument was a simple one: if the senses are the instruments by which we know the phenomena of the immediate world, how are we to know that which is *not* an object of the senses, if not through recollection?

What Plato proposed was that the past is immemorial, an existence in itself that is not "psychological" but ontological. Centuries later Bergson would refer back to this idea in order to resolve the issue of memory: "recollections do not have to be preserved anywhere other than in duration. *Recollection therefore is preserved in itself.*"[98] Our ability to remember is not dependent upon a series of associations but rather upon a "leap into being, into being-in-itself, into the being in itself of the past."[99] Or as Bergson wrote,

> "We become conscious of an act *sui generis* by which we detach ourselves from the present in order to replace ourselves, first in the past in general, then in a certain region of the past—a work of adjustment, something like the focusing of a camera. But our recollection still remains virtual. We simply prepare ourselves to receive it by adopting the appropriate attitude . . . from the virtual state it passes into the actual."[100]

What this means is that we do not need the concept of an unconscious to situate the phenomena of memory and meaning. Depth is not an "interior" experience, but rather the folded-over

---

[96]Gilles Deleuze, *Bergsonism*, New York: Zone Books, 1988, pp. 59, 58.

[97]*Phaedo*, 72e-77a.

[98]Deleuze, *Bergsonism*, p. 54. Deleuze's emphasis.

[99]*Ibid.*, p. 57.

[100]quoted in *Ibid.*, p. 56.

awareness of the activity that had occurred on the surface of experience, the between that delineates the experience of an "outside."

xiv.

The strategies created by multimillion dollar marketing programs depend on a theory of the unconscious to justify their procedures, to discover what subliminal technique, image, message, time of year, and wording should be used to best present and sell a specific product. About the business of the production of a social Eros, these strategies serve by guaranteeing that the fulfillment of your fabricated desire will appropriately define you to others: that your car, suit, dress, bag, watch, jeans (in addition to your sweet old etcs.), are the proper talismanic instruments for the power you wish to embody. It is in this manner (in a consumer society such as ours) that we become coded and controlled by our "owned" objects which serve to sign to others where we may be located along the lines of an invisible graph of stratifications and classifications of the conceptual person.

The normalization of modern Twentieth Century Western being—the cement that binds each member of society into a desired whole, where the concept of individuality is fulfilled only if you adapt to an idea (which is the conspiratorial nod of whichever aspect of the natural attitude you have adhered yourself to)—has passed out of the hands of religion as its major determining factor and into the hands of psychology, whose product (engineered to entice you) *is* the unconscious. It has made of this coding activity of language *a* language—psychology—which in turn informs us that we have an individual responsibility to that which encodes us—an unconscious.

This unconscious, we are told, is not only contained within each of us as something we have a moral responsibility towards, but that must also be continually policed by us. Whereas the Platonic doctrine informed us that the body was the prison of the soul, the Twentieth Century doctrine informs us that the unconscious is the ego's prison. Furthermore, we are told that in order to be free of this cell one must conform to the "natural" and inherent laws of the prison—that the unconscious as defined must be obeyed (if one is to expect release) by adapting oneself to what we must accept are its innate psychological principles. In modern parlance this release is coded as "the resolution of the Oedipal complex," "individuation," or just simply "transformation." To fly out of and above any such situation (as any ex-mental patient will confirm) one must conform. All transformations are confirmations of a policy. Such is the nature of the transfiguration that therapy as it is presently practiced provides. This theory of the unconscious recommends us all to a Gulag of guilt if one should not fit what is fitting:

> "The sting of a bad conscience even spurs you on to discover things that were unconscious before, and in this way you may be able to cross the threshold of the unconscious and take cognizance of those impersonal forces which make you an unconscious instrument of the wholesale murderer in man."[101]

In short, the theory of the unconscious is just that—a theory, an idea created to explain an activity of consciousness. The concept is, as Jung put it, "an assumption for the sake of convenience."[102] The location of this activity is not *in* psyche as a given, but in the collectivized dynamic of human beingness we call language. To be human is to be language. The term "the unconscious" (along with all similes to be discovered by comparative religion, philology, depth psychology, etc.) simply refers us to a coding activity of consciousness. It is not something other than consciousness, but the essence of consciousness' organizational activity. It is a process which when folded back on itself creates that Empedoclian roofed cavern of being[103], its dark operation we now call *an* unconscious.

The primary assumption behind our present-day theory of the unconscious is that there is an objective reality the clarity of which is obscured by each individual's personality and difficulties thereof as complicated by unresolved and unconscious issues. That is, Oedipal conflicts, anima/animus possessions, Mother-Father complexes, and all manner of other types of possessions ranging from

---

[101]Jung, *CW*, vol. 11, para. 86.

[102]*Ibid.*, para. 64.

[103]Freeman, *Ancilla*, Fragment 120, p. 65.

the simplicity of a bad attitude to the complexity of genetically transmitted moral values that get in the way of our truly being present to the world and all of its workings.[104]

What we must allow is that simply because certain types of experience cannot be identified as consciousness does not mean that they are not in and of consciousness. This might simply mean that we have not yet fully recognized what consciousness is, much less fully comprehended its operations. It is one thing to postulate hypothetically the existence of a dimension called the unconscious, and quite another to make of the hypothesis an undeniable fact—which is exactly what has happened since Freud's original formulation. By never questioning the validity of this hypothesis we not only strengthen our convictions concerning what consciousness is, but we therefore see no reason to recognize the possibility that what we call the unconscious is simply our ignorance concerning the true nature of consciousness.

Merleau-Ponty suggested this when he stated that the concept of the unconscious could cover only an "unrecognised, unformulated knowledge, that we do not wish to assume." He added to this

> "In an approximate language, Freud is on the point of discovering what other thinkers have more appropriately named *ambiguous perception*. It is by working in this direction that we shall find a civil status for this consciousness which brushes its objects (eluding them at the moment it is going to designate them, and taking account of them as the blind man takes account of obstacles rather than recognising them), which does not want to know about them (which does not know about them, to the extent that it knows about them, and knows about them to the extent that it does not know about them), and which subtends our express acts and understandings."[105]

Such misrepresentation is what lies behind the issue of self-deception. With the dissemination of psychoanalytic thought throughout our culture during the better portion of this century,

---

[104]Jung, *CW*, vol. 8, para. 673.

[105]Merleau-Ponty, *Signs*, Richard McCleary, trans., Evanston, Ill.: Northwestern University Press, 1964, pp. 229-30.

this supposed tendency or proclivity on the part of individuals to deceive themselves has become an assumed operation of the psyche. To take for granted that this phenomenon is an inherent and universal property of consciousness is to overlook the possibility that it may solely be a jural quality of certain types of cultures. That is, self-deception is a mechanism whereby an individual may be held responsible for an action while at the same time remaining blameless. As we shall see in a later section self-deception is a psychological quality peculiar to a guilt culture, and is the category into which the Western World fits. A therapy that operates as if self-deception is an *a priori* attribute of the psyche will also be a technique that essentially punctuates, if not inculcates, a cultural attribute that is *symptomatic* of a peculiar and punitive concept of the person.

That consciousness can present its operation to itself in this manner, that it can anticipate its own needs to the extent of sometimes denying its own needs—that it can *actually move against its own nature*, which is to *become*, in order to be, and to allow this becoming to be suppressed in favor of its own continuity of experience is the miracle, the mystery, and the contradiction that so puzzles us in our search for personal meaning: that *to be* in the general sense, in the sense of the natural attitude, is sometimes to deny.

By locating the origin of pathology in a dimension defined as different from consciousness one is diverted from the actual operations of consciousness. It is only by recognizing the cultural specificity of pathologies that we shall be able to learn more about the operations of consciousness. But as long as we divert the cause of pathology to an unconscious realm all that is accomplished when turning to it (which, I repeat, is simply a metaphor for our lack of knowledge concerning the nature of consciousness) is the reconciliation of the individual with societal directives that initiated the pathology in the first place—that is, a normalization process whose sole aim is the creation of a social-person.

XV.

Of course, one could argue here that language simply allows us to describe an *a priori* dimension containing both interiority and subjectivity wherein "depth" exists as a given.[106] Looked at from this perspective psychological "depth" gains its dimensionality the further away from the surface of phenomenal reality consciousness moves. In other words, in the language and inevitable rationale of present-day depth psychology, we achieve depth only by descending *into* the unconscious, which we all suppose lies at the base of subjective reality.[107] We are told that a movement in depth allows us to decode and evaluate experience. The implication here is that depth is a property to be discovered only by a distancing of oneself from immediate experience in order to better understand the very experience one moves away from. No further comment is needed here.

One can further argue that any definition of subjectivity elected by a culture simply gives shape or form to an existing *a priori* subjectivity—that an inner dimension exists which need simply be arranged by language. The fallacy of this position is found in the assumption that one *a priori*, (in this instance, subjectivity) can be changed or altered by another *a priori* (in this instance, language). But this would be a contradiction, for the very essence of the *a priori* is its eternal consistency as a principle of unalterability. Thus, language could not shape an *a priori* "subjectivity." Language creates subjectivity.

The most immediately significant fold the world makes to incorporate us is language. The horizon cannot be folded over without the language which defines "horizon" along with all of the coordinates that are implied in its definition: above, below, over, under, behind, in front of, left, right, etc. It is the peripheral recognition of concepts given us by language's reality that allows us consistently to locate ourselves in a manner congruent with the reality of others.

---

[106]cf. Jung, *CW*, vol. 18, para. 1159, where the personal and collective unconscious are discussed as "layers."

[107]Jung, *CW*, vol. 12, paras. 463-67

If it is language that creates the experience of subjectivity, then one's thinking of subjectivity is actually an activity that language performs upon itself. Subjectivity is therefore not a condition, but an activity of language—for desire is consciousness, the verb "to be".

xvi.

It has been suggested that the three foldings of body, power, and the Outside might possibly have served as the matrix of the Western psyche, leaving open the possibility that they might also constitute the manner by which consciousness generally apprehends the phenomenon of the world and comes to the experience of subjectivity. This could explain why several divergently different world-cultures share mythological cosmogonies constructed upon markedly similar parameters—specifically the three-tiered or layered universe. To understand such cultural parallelisms as being the products of an archetypal way of seeing—an organizational and perceptual inevitability that is genetically transmitted—we would have to assume the existence of a transcendental ego that eternally organizes phenomenal experience. In other words, we would have to assume a primordial consciousness that we are an object of, and that all of our actions are therefore predetermined in that they are but the thinking of a transcendent consciousness, a soliloquy of deity itself generated out of a primordial language specific to its own site. Humanity would then be but a likely story, a fiction generated by a transcendent truth, an uttered sentence.

I have proceeded from the position that it is not the psyche which organizes phenomena, but rather that phenomena organize the psyche. The legitimations necessary for the continued and necessary reorganizations that a culture experiences over the course of history are a function of the fourth fold—the fold of knowledge. The remainder of this work will concern itself with the origin of the knowledge psychology has appropriated, and the methods by which it applies such knowledge as truth.

Implicit in such an approach will be the implication that we must address all studies produced (up until this time and this time included) that speak of archetypes and their relation to the issue of psychology. We must not divorce ourselves from these issues of the archetype, but must instead press forward into the imaginations that have been generated by the concept. The value of the archetype is that it reveals to us precisely where a specific value has become rigidified, codified, and static—where life has been submitted to the limitations of formulaic images after which all responses must be patterned. The archetype shows us how the power of a value system has been organized to produce a truth in as palpable and convincing a manner as human ingenuity can devise. In short, it mirrors to us the artistry behind our ability to experience the paradoxical condition of self-deception. This is exactly the value of the archetype: it shows us what about ourselves we have misunderstood, and how such a misunderstanding is placed in the laps of gods so that we might escape our responsibility towards our own becoming.

If we can accurately distinguish each utterance made regarding an archetype, identifying it with those places in a culture where its defined dynamic is operative, then we can begin to understand what conditions necessitate the fictionalization of social phenomena. The emergence of a myth, whether it be ancient or modern, could then be approached as indicative of an ambiguous perception of a social event in the midst of legitimating a position *that can only persist as long as the ambiguity is maintained*. I might mention in passing that dreams could also be approached in this manner.

Instead of looking through the surface to discover the fiction of the surface reflected back at us, an anthropology and sociology of the archetype could be developed that would bring the surface (and therefore the world) into sharper focus. This then would arrive at a depth that has not been folded: an apprehension and appreciation of the immediacy and relevance of the activity occurring on the surface of the body of experience.

Part II

Original Sin

"My guiding principle is this: Guilt is never to be doubted."
Franz Kafka, *The Penal Colony*

"You will be required to do wrong no matter where you go. It is the basic condition of life, to be required to violate your own identity . . . It is the ultimate shadow, the defeat of creation."
Philip K. Dick, *Do Androids Dream of Electric Sheep?*

"In such psychological cruelty we see an insanity of the will that is without parallel: man's will to find himself guilty, and unredeemably so."
Friedrich Nietzsche, *The Genealogy of Morals*

i.

The incidence of foldings that lead to the experience of subjectivity outlined in Part I may at this juncture appear to be but an arbitrary and abstract invention, thereby contradicting my opening statements that any investigation into the nature of consciousness must arise out of the investigation of the experience of natural phenomena. Before proceeding further, it will therefore be necessary that I offer an at least cursory accounting of the manner by which such foldings occur out of the psyche's responses to being.

Nietzsche had observed that all of our mental processes—thinking, feeling, willing, remembering—could occur without their becoming a datum of consciousness. That is, without their entering into the domain of selective awareness, the realm of sustained comprehension.[108] We could lead our lives as Kafkaian dogs, acting, responding, without the sense of a continuity of experience so necessary to that condition we call consciousness. As Nietzsche puts it, "The whole of life would be possible without, as it were, seeing itself in a mirror."[109] That much of life, of personal experience and acts, does indeed proceed in this manner need not be argued. Life is habitual, an aggregation of habits that in time become as necessary as the blinking of our eyelids. But if life can be lived like this, why then does the state called consciousness arise in the first place? Why have humans not led the life of earthworms following the simple course of their needs? Nietzsche's answer is simple and direct: "*Consciousness has developed only under the pressure of the need for communication.*"[110]

---

[108]Friedrich Nietzsche, *The Gay Science*, Walter Kaufmann, trans., New York: Vintage Books, 1974, Section 354, p. 297.

[109]*Ibid.*

[110]*Ibid.*, Section 354, p. 298. Nietzsche's emphasis.

Consciousness has come into existence because of a need humans have that is absent in other creatures. This need is the expression of what could actually be called a deficiency, the product (more than likely) of a mutation that sharply demarcated humans from other orders of life. While discussing Peter Berger's thesis concerning the construction of social reality, I addressed this issue in an earlier work:

> "[Berger] explains that the society-building . . . peculiar to humanity is based upon the fact that the human world is an open system, as opposed to the non-human world which is predestined by highly specialized and directed instincts and thereby contained and closed. Thus, the non-human world is a biologically determined reality in contrast to the human world which, while on the one hand sharing certain common features with the non-human world, also has at its disposal a certain quantum of free will."[111]

It is because humans are the most endangered species (our ability at adaptation being but the result of a necessary compensation and *not* a matter of our genetic inheritance), needing the cooperation and aid of others to survive, and therefore in need of a method by which we may communicate this need, that consciousness came into existence. But before such need may be articulated the specific nature of the distress must be known so that it may be named.[112] The need for a language to communicate, and language's need for specificity, forced us to not simply experience but to investigate the outcome of experience. It was in only such a manner that we could correctly express and communicate our expectations of the moment. This, more than likely, was the manner by which self-awareness came to pass, forcing us to create communication skills a millionfold more complex (and therefore of another order) than the genetically-transmitted "language" of dancing bees or of hierarchically ordered ant colonies. Consciousness is therefore reactive, growing out of the need to communicate the organism's responses to phenomena:

---

[111]Poncé, *Working the Soul,* pp. 142-3.

[112]Nietzsche, *The Gay Science,* section 354, p. 298.

"The 'evolution' of a thing, a custom, an organ is thus by no means its *progressus* toward a goal, even less a logical *progressus* by the shortest route and with the smallest expenditure of force—but a succession of more or less profound, more or less mutually independent processes of subduing, plus the resistances they encounter, the attempts at transformation for the purpose of defense and reaction, and the results of successful counteractions. The form is fluid, but the 'meaning' is even more so."[113]

This relation of active and reactive forces that the organism brings to the experience of phenomena, along with the reactive and restrictive value-building activity of society, acts upon the instincts to the point where they may become modified. However, as Nietzsche (as Freud and Jung punctuate in following his lead) noted,

" . . . instincts that do not discharge themselves outwardly *turn inward—[to create the]* . . . *internalization* of man . . . The entire inner world, originally as thin as if it were stretched between two membranes, expanded and extended itself, acquired depth, breadth, and height, in the same measure as outward discharge was *inhibited*."[114]

Despite Nietzsche's use of spatial terminology to describe the dynamics of modified instincts as an activity of interiority—occurring within a "space"—(but in agreement with our earlier observations that such terminology was what gave rise to the coordinates by which we construct the experience of subjectivity), what he has described is the process by which foldings occur. One can only assume (but for this instance of the spatialization of organic and psychological processes) he meant just that when he wrote:

"Oh, those Greeks! They knew how to live. What is required for that is to stop courageously at the surface, the fold, the skin, to adore appearance, to believe in forms, tones, words, in the whole Olympus of appearance. Those Greeks were superficial—*out of profundity*."[115]

---

[113]Nietzsche, *On the Genealogy of Morals*, Walter Kaufmann, New York: Vintage Books, 1969, II, section 12, pp. 77-78.

[114]*Ibid.*, section 16, p. 84. Nietzsche's emphasis.

[115]Nietzsche, *The Gay Science*, p. 38. Nietzsche's emphasis. I am indebted to Tom Steele for bringing this quote to my attention.

The assignment of an *a priori* and spatially defined interiority to the experience of subjectivity discussed earlier—inevitably leading to the concept "internalization"—is not only unnecessary to describe psychological phenomena, but misleading. It is misleading because the objects of "internalization"—i.e., the experiences of the individual—are then given a prominence over and above the socially constructed value systems that shaped the experiences themselves. Too often, so-called internalized realities, when they are diagnostically determined as skewed, are understood as the result of some innately aberrant quality of the individual. That is, moral and ethical judgements are made on the basis of the belief that the cause of psychological difficulty is a matter of the individual's inherent nature.

For example, we are told that

> "The ego is more or less constantly threatened from three directions: (1) the objective reality of the outer world; (2) the severity of archaic and infantile conscience (superego); and (3) the urgent impulsive and compulsive power of instinctual drives."[116]

Ego strength, the prerequisite of normality, ultimately is measured by the ability of an individual in meeting and defending himself from these three hazardous conditions. Normality is therefore a stable but plastic state of resistance, its strength determined by "the effectiveness with which the ego discharges its various functions [in the face of the above three threats]."[117] It is for this reason that, in the final analysis, the ability of an individual to either withstand or be overcome by a traumatic event is understood within the context of his ego strength or defenses. (That the modern Western definition of the person and normality is based upon the idea of defensive strength in the face of hazardous conditions will be discussed in greater detail during the next few pages.)

In addition, the assumptions regarding the *a priori* nature of subjectivity embody the idea of a genetically transmitted morality in both Freud's and Jung's psychologies. Freud's position that the development of a conscience is incumbent upon the existence of

---

[116]Hinsie/Leland, *Psychiatric Dictionary,* p. 255.

[117]*Ibid.,* p. 256.

a penis and the ensuing fear of castration is but one of the many results of this position.[118] Conscience, tradition tells us, is the product of a morally correct personality. The existence of a ruminative and *internal* process of thinking directed towards a consideration of values, we are again told, is what constitutes a socially sanctioned conscience. But, if we follow Freud's logic, it is the dominance of a male or female gene that ultimately determines the possibility of conscience. Jung's contributions to the idea of an *a priori* is found in his position that the goal of therapy is the restoration of a genetically transmitted archetype of wholeness.[119] In both instances biology determines the structure and dynamics of internalized realities. Where this, and other assumptions regarding the nature of the psyche, are not openly stated in psychological discourse, they are nonetheless generally assumed in the practice of therapy and counselling. Such is the result of the thesis regarding the existence of an *a priori* "internal" reality.

Instead to see the experience of subjectivity as the result of a folding of social reality, an invagination of values extended as meanings, is not to absolve the individual of ethical and moral determinations. It in fact places a greater demand upon the individual to recognize that the condition he identifies himself with as consciousness is actually a reactive phenomenon based upon a defensive posture towards being.[120] In short, consciousness is one of many psychological functions and not the sole and primary objective of being *par excellance*. Or, as Jung simply put it, the ego

---

[118]"Under the impression of the danger of losing his penis, the Oedipus complex [in a young boy] is abandoned, repressed and, in the most normal cases, entirely destroyed . . . and a severe super-ego is set up as its heir. What happens with a girl is almost the opposite . . . In the absence of fear of castration the chief motive is lacking which leads boys to surmount the Oedipus complex . . . In these circumstances the formation of the super-ego must suffer; it cannot attain the strength and independence which give it its cultural significance, and feminists are not pleased when we point out to them the effects of this factor upon the average feminine character." Sigmund Freud, *New Introductory Lectures on Psychoanalysis*, New York: W. W. Norton & Company, Inc., 1964, Lecture XXXIII, p. 129.

[119]Jung, *CW*, vol. 9ii, para. 73.

[120]cf. Nietzsche, *The Gay Science*, pp. 299-300.

is but one of *many* complexes.[121] Consciousness is a psychic apparatus by which being may access itself—the "itself" being nothing more than its own becoming. As an apparatus, consciousness cannot claim itself to be either an idealized goal or the major intent of becoming.

It is *becoming* that should become the focus of any therapy seeking to move beyond the socialization demands therapy itself has until this time aligned itself with—the "knowledge" that is no knowledge, but a position regarding the nature of being. Consciousness understood as a *function* of the psyche rather than an exalted condition might then properly discover a process of evaluation that is not dependent upon the natural attitude's socially prescribed and coded techniques for the establishment of values. Then and only then may we fully come to understand the potential of consciousness as the discriminatory tool it is, releasing it from techniques and tactics that seek to maintain it as a *status quo* function, and freeing it so that it might begin to fulfill the inherent exploratory nature of becoming.

ii.

I pick up the trail of this knowledge-fold on the Greek side of the historical fence because it was they who, through a reorganization of the cosmos, first made the leap from mythological to philosophical thinking. This event occurred during the second half of the Fifth Century with the breakdown of Hesiod's cosmogony and its gradual replacement by the cosmos of philosophy. It has been noted that when such a breakdown occurs, "an autonomous ethic appears . . . 'Autonomous' . . . [denoting] an ethic in which sufficing reasons for moral action can be given without invoking divine sanctions or sanctions from any other aspect of the cosmogony."[122]

---

[121]Jung, *CW*, vol. 18, para. 149.

[122]Aruthur W. H. Adkins, "Ethics and the Breakdown of the Cosmogony in Ancient Greece," in Robin W. Lovin and Frank E. Reynolds, editors, *Cosmogony and Ethical Order,* Chicago and London: The University of Chicago Press, 1985, p. 279.

A cosmogony that is mythological in presentation is the storied structure of a group's or society's dispensation of rules and rights. Thus, the hierarchically-tiered world of the Hesiodic period reflected the transmitted Mycenaean concept of monarchy.[123] Anaximander replaced this with the image of a cosmos in which symmetry and equality ordered and governed. From that point on the universe would no longer be depicted as a dimension marked by the absolute opposition of high and low, by "cosmic levels that differentiated the divine powers, and whose spatial directions had contrasting religious meanings."[124] The monarchically ordered universe came to an end. *Dike* (Justice) no longer acted on behalf of a sovereign power, but instead sought to maintain equilibrium between contrasting but equal powers. No one element—such as Thales' water, Anaximenes' air, or Heraclitus' fire—would rule the other elemental powers. Each would have to "make reparation to one another for their injustice" should such an attempt occur.[125]

The fold of the Outside was given greater extension and dimensionality by Anaximander's assigning of demarcating distances to the originating qualities (hot, cold, wet, dry) and their elements (fire, air, water, earth), as well as to the size and distance of the planets.[126] The exacting astronomy of the Babylonians transmitted to the Greeks had been purely mathematical.[127] That is, the mathematical predictability of astronomical events did not depend upon geometry, or an imagination that located these movements within a three-dimensional space. One could say that the Babylonians more than likely imaged the background of the starry heavens as one-dimensional, the planets and stars sliding across

---

[123]cf. Martin P. Nilsson, *The Mycenaean Origin of Greek Mythology*, Emily Vermeule, trans., Berkeley, Los Angeles, London: University of California Press, 1972, pp. 250-1.

[124]Jean-Pierre Vernant, *The Origins of Greek Thought*, Ithaca, New York: Cornell University Press, 1982, p. 121.

[125]Freeman, *Ancilla*, Anaximander, frag. 1.

[126]Kathleen Freeman, *Companion to the Pre-Socratic Philosophers*, Cambridge, Mass.: Harvard University Press, 1966, pp. 60-1.

[127]O. Neugebauer, *The Exact Sciences in Antiquity*, Providence, R.I.: Brown University Press, 1970, p. 10 ff.

its surface. Anaximander's cosmology changed all of that. His geometry of a dimensional and equilibrated cosmos would in time become the matrix for the political organization of a city based upon egalitarian law and order. Dimensionality would translate itself into the socially defined distances between rules and rights of order, and equality into the tangential gradations of the social person differentiated out of the cultural and psychological persons. In short (in this latter instance), the judicial determinations concerning the nature of equality were only applied to the social person. As we shall see, this fold of the Outside onto the social world of Hellenistic Greece would be pressed further by Plato's theory of the soul. The dissemination of this new image of the cosmos was on the one hand literally displayed to the public by the creation of mechanical models of the universe,[128] and on the other by open philosophical discourse. The reorganization of the cosmos by Anaximander constitutes the substance of the fold of knowledge that has given the Western psyche its peculiar structure.

The theories of the soul, along with the methods by which it should be organized and maintained, no longer depended upon ritual sacrifice and religious obeisance. Philosophy took the reigns of the soul in hand, and its study came under the direction of men dialoguing in schools and academies. Training in these matters preceded discourse and practice. The Twentieth Century saw a revival of this type of education with Freud's founding of his school of thought. As Ellenberger has observed, the training analysis of Freud's school followed the lines of initiation these earlier schools demanded:

> "Not only does the training analysis demand a heavy financial sacrifice, but also a surrender of privacy and of the whole self. By this means a follower is integrated into the Society more indissolubly than ever was a Pythagorian, Stoic, or Epicurean in his own organization. We are thus led to view Freud's most striking

---

[128]Anaximander was not only credited with the creation of the first map of the world, but also with the creation of a sphere showing the geometric structure of the cosmos. cf. W.K.C. Guthrie, F.B.A., *A History of Greek Philosophy*, London, New York, Melbourne: Cambridge University Press, 1977, Vol. I, p. 74, and Freeman, *Companion*, p. 63

achievement in the revival of the Greco-Roman type of philosophical schools."[129]

In addition, Stoicism, along with the fundamental concept of the Logos borrowed from Heraclitus,[130] runs throughout Freud's thought. The Heraclitean subordination of the individual to the law of nature, or the Logos, parallels Freud's mechanistic thesis that there is a natural law of the psyche that governs all mental processes:

> "This ordered universe (*cosmos*), which is the same for all, was not created by any one of the gods or of mankind, but it was ever and is and shall be ever-living Fire, kindled in measure and quenched in measure."[131]

Jung in essence agreed with Freud's hierarchical structuring of the psyche and the intent of the psychological logos, adding to them Heraclitus' theory of *enantiodromia* ("return to the opposite"), which he translated into the self-regulatory function of certain mental processes.[132]

---

[129]Ellenberger, *The Discovery of the Unconscious*, New York: Basic Books, Inc., 1970, p. 550.

[130]For a detailed discussion of Freud's psychology as a cosmogony, I recommend the reader to Lee H. Yearley, "Freud as Creator and Critic of Cosmogonies and Their Ethics," in Lovin and Reynolds, *Cosmogony*, pp. 381-413.

[131]Freeman, *Ancilla*, Heraclitus frag. 30. As Ellenberger states, however, Freud is more aligned with the Epicurean aim of the removal of anxiety, whereas it is Adler's position that is most suggestive of Stoic influence. cf., Henri F. Ellenberger, *Discovery*, pp. 42, 635, 648.

[132]"I use the term enantiodromia for the emergence of the unconscious opposite in the course of time. This characteristic phenomenon practically always occurs when an extreme, one-sided tendency dominates conscious life; in time an equally powerful counterposition is set up, which first inhibits the conscious performance and subsequently breaks through the conscious control." C. G. Jung, *CW*, vol. 6, para. 709.

"The mysterious phenomenon of the spontaneous reversal of regression was experienced by all those who passed successfully through a creative illness and has become a characteristic feature of Jungian synthetic-hermeneutic therapy." Ellenberger, *Discovery*, p. 713.

It is of interest to note here, as an aside, that the harmony Heraclitus speaks of is actually the tension that exists between the opposites:

But it is the central thesis of Anaximander's thought that lies at the heart of Jung's schemata of the human psyche—the four functions and the archetype of the self. Anaximander proposed the existence of a discrete and infinite substance, the *aperion*, or unlimited, "the original material of existing things . . . the source from which existing things derive their existence."[133] It was from this *prima materia*, that the four elements were expressed as reciprocal opposition, all "equal in power."[134]

Jung defines the archetype of the self as timeless and as having existed before any birth, adding that by this he does not mean to put forward "a metaphysical statement but a psychological fact."[135] As the *aperion*, the self also gives rise to four fundamental expressions of itself—the four functions of feeling, thinking, sensation, and intuition.[136] These functions are defined in terms of their conflictual opposition (rational/irrational) in addition to the compensatory powers of extraversion and introversion. While their total differentiation can never be achieved[137] (for this would lead to a state of perfection comparable to a god's), the goal of therapy is nonetheless a movement towards the condition of their total differentiation—the archetype of the self.

These (and other comparisons that must be put off for another time) form the knowledge that presently enfolds psychology. Almost all of this knowledge has its beginnings in the Greek theory of the cosmos that by the term's very definition informs us

---

"They do not understand how that which differs with itself is in agreement: harmony consists of opposing tension, like that of a bow and the lyre." (Freeman, *Ancilla*, Heraclitus, frag. 51.)

In accordance with this Heraclitean position one can only assume that psychological harmony is achieved through the conflictual dynamic that arises between the unconscious and consciousness. That is, harmony can be known only through the experience of tension, or at the very least a persistent awareness of the *idea* of a conflictual condition, of a state of truce, perpetual readiness, and defense.

[133]Freeman, *Ancilla*, Anaximander, frag. 1.

[134]Aristotle, *Meteorology*, I, 340a 16.

[135]Jung, *CW*, vol. 16, para. 378 & footnote #31.

[136]Jung, *CW*, vol. 5, para. 611.

[137]Jung, *CW* 18, para. 212.

of the concept of an ordering and pre-existent activity. Theory constructs—it is an activity whose proof is the discovery of what it
intends to discover: *itself* imbedded as fact in the "hidden" dimension of phenomena, as that which knows it exists but has forgotten
where to find itself, an echo that never had a voice. No theory can
escape this condition. But it is exactly at the juncture where theory
(specifically theory dealing with ontological questions) arranges
the world to fulfill itself that psychology should attend. The price
that had to be paid for the transition from Hesiodic mythologizing
to Anaximanderian cosmogonizing was the idea that becoming
must be continually compensated; that the damage done to the
aperion (to the *a priori* self) by the birth of being could only be
repaired by eternal reparation.

iii.

In the final analysis, a cursory meditation on the meaning of
person reveals that we are at the very least referring to three different types of persons. The first, shaped through social interaction,
is the cultural person, composed of the amalgamation of the
peculiarities that distinguish one culture from another—the differences in body type, movement, emotional reaction, gesticulation,
and all other mannerisms that identify us as members of a specific
group. Almost always, these are the aspects of ourselves which
take several generations to wear off.

The second is the social-person which is essentially constructed with the cooperation of other selves reacting and acting
towards one another in society. This person comes into being
through the type of self-reflection that seeks to imitate and/or com-
plement the way other people in our group are acting. It is in this
sense that the second person is socially constructed by the opinions
and expectations of social intercourse. Whereas the cultural person
comes to embody his society's meaning, ideas, and values, the
social person embodies and personifies his society's rules of
relationship, the laws that control social action. The relation that
one has towards oneself is based upon what one learns because
of one's relations with an other or others. We come to know ourselves through our perception of what others perceive *as* us. The
degree that my response to the other's gaze causes me to adjust,

edit, or revise myself in action is the degree to which myself as a *person* is socially constructed. The relationship that I have with myself is composed of the relationship others have with me.

While cultural and social-persons are constructed out of the types of responses necessary to facilitate commerce and communication with others—both linguistic and non-linguistic languages— the third person is essentially a metaphysical construct. This being is constructed out of the ontological answers to existence one's culture finds necessary for the creation and maintenance of a sense of meaning—those answers that assure us there is a reason for being, and explain why all of the peculiarities of being came into existence in the first place. Every meaning, however, is the result of valuation. That is, meanings are the refined or aestheticized products of value-systems. One cannot agree or disagree with a meaning without the process of valuation. Values story themselves in meaning, and such stories are metaphysical in that they presume the existence of an ultimate value, a transcendent or archetypal ego/self.

Every culture and society in the past and present construct such a metaphysic to explain themselves to themselves, and it is by such explanations that individuals develop a sense of kinship which allows them to bond with others in their group. It is under such a metaphysical banner that unity of meaning and purpose is accessed by each member of a culture and society. In the past, this metaphysic, this explanation of being, was ostensibly offered us in the tenets of religion. But every metaphysic at some point or another is placed in jeopardy by the discovery or conjecture of other possible explanations of meaning, at which time the prevailing metaphysic either falls completely out of favor or adapts itself to the new meanings. The fall of the Classical world in the face of Christianity is an example of the former situation, while the adjustment of Church science to the Copernican revelation is an example of the latter.

Here a far more important problem arises: if an individual's psyche and sense of self has been constructed in the manner I have described, then the experiences of interiorization, reflection, and contemplation are actually vehicles by which we turn *towards* the world to the entire extent that these structures are of the world. Nietzsche seems to have intimated as much when he wrote:

"Consciousness does not really belong to man's individual existence but rather to his social or herd nature . . . Consequently, given the best will in the world to understand ourselves as individually as possible, 'to know ourselves,' each of us will always succeed in becoming conscious only of what is not individual but 'average.' Our thoughts themselves are continually governed by the character of consciousness—by the 'genius of the species' that commands it—and translated back into the perspective of the herd."[138]

Where then is the "myself" in all of this if what I turn towards when I turn towards myself is the imprint of the world on my gaze and in my gaze? How do I see myself if what I look at myself with is a way of thinking rather than a direct and simple looking, which is either a forgotten way of looking or a looking that has not yet been discovered? And what of this "interior" where I locate myself? Is it not simply an interstice created by the overlapping outlines of the constructed persons, a space defined even before we locate it? When I turn towards myself if what I find there is a socially constructed "I" then my thinking occurs within the objects of the world which are the substance of my thought. In other words, my thinking is not about the Outside but *of* the Outside, composed of and structured by the Outside. It is the inside of the Outside, and not of a "my inside."

What groups know of the Outside is the image Jung called the collective unconscious, the image that they have of the world that is retained for them in language as it exists in the social world: it is the archetype called the unconscious. As pointed out earlier, Jung meant by this term a process distinct from but compensatory to consciousness. My suggestion (that it is not something distinct from consciousness but consciousness itself) simply punctuates the observation that consciousness represents its own justifications as being not only something other than itself but something that transcends itself. What we call self-deception is the incorporation of the intending activity of consciousness, the folding of intentionality that then posits the existence of something *other* than itself. It is this divinization of intentionality that creates symbols, of which the individual is but one.

---

[138]Nietzsche, *The Gay Science*, p. 299.

What we must take note of here is that these three persons are created by the restraining forces of institutional values as truths regarding what the lineaments of each person should look like. The triune nature of the individual is the amalgamation of constraints and restraints that he has been taught are the inevitable conditions for inclusion in social existence. Refusals or inabilities to agree with these values (which I have explained earlier are actually forces) are what are referred to as "symptoms" or pathologies.

Failure to resolve the tensions and conflicts generated by these three persons, to create a self and individual whose identity is based upon such resolution, results in states of consciousness deemed pathological. The goal of therapy as it is presently practiced is one of educating the individual in the resolution or management of conflictual states. The "internalization" of and identification with institutions, along with the conflicts they generate, then become the responsibility of the person. He is taught to believe that the resolution of the conflicts he has accepted as personal and subjective will be achieved by the self-knowledge gained through self-inquiry. But if self-inquiry is simply a focusing in on, review, and adjustment of the socially constructed persons the individual embodies, then all that is achieved by such technique is the maintenance of that which has produced the conflict in the first place. The individual becomes inured to his experience of suffering via a technique that "adjusts" (i.e., normalizes) him to a concept of health or wholeness. This adjustment can only occur through the deification of the autonomous nature of society-building, which then leads to legitimation, justification, and culture-specific "truths." It is in this manner that the politic of the natural attitude maintains itself. The individual so created is but a personification of society's legitimating procedures. The techniques aimed at maintaining the legitimation of a culture's perspective during the course of its existence seek to create an individual who exemplifies the "inherent" truth of its institutions.

Lacan has stressed that the child's ego is imaginary in that it is based upon expectations originating outside of itself—a simulation of what his mother wishes him to become. I would extend this proposal beyond the mirror of mothering to include all three persons outlined above as the products of a combined simulation. To that extent, the concept of the individual is also an imaginary construct. As Lacan observed, this identification with an idealized ego is the cause of narcissism, and therefore is "just another word for humanism; since the primary purpose of bourgeois society is the provision of supposedly self-sufficient individuals. The imaginary thus serves as a repository of the falsehoods of the 'self' at both a psychological and social level."[139]

But the question we are left with is, what is the origin of the parent's image of the child's imaginary self that must be consistently in agreement with other selves if not with the three persons described above? The parent is carrier of the idealized image of the self society has demanded compliance with. The parent's failures, intended or not, to comply fully with the idealized image of the person—an image so perfect, an archetype, that its very nature defies fulfillment—are also passed on to the child. It is this tripartite construct of the person that is proposed in those psychologies, religions, philosophies, and metaphysics that stipulate the goal of life is the realization of an ideal, an Absolute and archetypal self accessed only by the disciplinary programs that constitute their dogma.

iv.

To date, it is understood that the Greek concept of the person as a social category, a figure composed of moral responsibilities and jural rights, an actor following a script, underwent its major revision at the hands of the Stoics. It was their concept of individual freedom, coupled with the introduction of the idea of personal (as contrasted with civil) conscience, that eventually led to the development of the idea of the person as a unity based upon the emendations of Christianity. And there the matter came to a halt, "our own notion of the human person . . . still basically [being] the Christian one."[140]

---

[139]Richard Kearney, *The Wake of Imagination*, Minneapolis: University of Minnesota Press, 1988, p. 259.

[140]Marcel Mauss, "A category of the human mind: the notion of person; the notion of self," in M. Carrithers, S. Collins, S. Lukes, editors, *The Category of the Person: Anthropology, philosophy, history*, Cambridge: Cambridge University Press, 1987, p. 19.

All religions and psychologies (if not every socially constructed reality) either implicitly or explicitly command a theory and definition of the person. However, in that every such theory also carries with it an implicit statement regarding what a true or appropriate person is, we inevitably end up with an image of the ideal person, an absolute—and, also inevitably, a statement to the effect that the person is an *a priori* condition, a condition whose end has already been established and whose realization can be achieved only by a technique. All religious and metaphysical systems—many of which incorporate the justifying proofs of a philosophy—offer rigorous programs tailored to the realization of this ideal person. Invariably, such systems are legalistic and punitive. Failure to achieve the ideal is deemed either symptomatic of moral imperfection, or cause for exclusion.

The earlier philosophical endeavor to resuscitate the ideal person through epistemological and dialogal techniques remains with us in the techniques of therapy—and the endeavor is still grounded in a perspective that demands we understand consciousness as a given psychic structure. Behind this idea is another which holds that there is an ultimate referent of thought, a consciousness standing over and above our human and everyday consciousness which is the ground of what we experience ourselves as being. It is from this Absolute that the idealized image of the person is derived.

In Western philosophy the concept of the Absolute refers us to that which, while not of this world, is in some manner nevertheless implicated in this world. Invariably, we are told to accept that its implication in being is as the ground and reason of being. The model of the person is either to be found in the Absolute as archetype, or in structures assigned to us by the Absolute. But by locating the Absolute in a distant and other-worldly dimension *beyond* the activity of the everyday we victimize being to a limitation, to a quest whose goal can only be realized through the imagery or fact of death, spiritual or mundane. Under such terms, our completion is not of this world, and not in the consciousness by which we know the world—our completion is unknown to us in the immediate experience of being. This development of the concept of the person in the West has progressed by delineations, emendations, and revisions that have only recently led to the concept of a psychological person. But this person psychology concerns itself with is but the patina of the metaphysical person constructed over these past several centuries. Therapy as it is presently practiced is but an extension of programs that seek to limit access to avenues of knowledge concerning the self, or of consciousness as it is given limited that it might be.

V.

Our word "person" is taken from the Latin *personae*, originally derived from the Greek *prosopeion*, both words meaning "mask." The Greek term for "mask" was itself originally derived from "*prosopon*, towards (*pros*) the eye, the face (*opa*)."[141] This "wearing of a face" points us to the theatrical use of masks to portray the *dramatis personaes* of the Greek theater. In other words, the original sense of the word "person" was that of role-playing, of the presentation of a stylized and immediately identifiable type of self that was given constancy through a story. The term at no time referred to an awareness of self, only of a social actor fulfilling a role. An awareness of self demands the concept of introspection that scholars have for some time conjectured first appeared in St. Augustine's allusion to such in his *De Trinitate*, completed in 417 A.D.[142] However, Momigliano presents a convincing argument against this thesis when he refers us to the fact that autobiographical treatises (which are the products of introspection) are found in the Fourth Century B.C., but in a form we tend to not think of as autobiographical.[143] These texts were speeches that had been presented in self-defense, "conditioned, if not determined, by the accusations of . . . enemies."[144] It was out of the defended presen-

---

[141]Eric Patridge, *Origins: A Short Etymological Dictionary of Modern English*, New York: Greenwich House, 1983, p. 487.

[142]cf. William Lyons, *The Disappearance of Introspection*, Cambridge, Mass., London: The MIT Press, 1968, p. 1.

[143]cf. A. Momigliano, "Marcel Mauss and the quest for the person in Greek biography and autobiography," in Carrithers, *The Category of the Person*, pp. 82-92.

[144]*Ibid.*, p. 90

tations of self that the concept of autobiography slowly developed, and from this the concept of the individual as an introspective being.[145] But the original concept of the person as framed by the early Greeks had not reached this stage of development—and it is was theirs that initially gave shape to ours in the Twentieth Century. The purpose of the person was to fulfill the story, to play out the drama.

The persons symbolized by the masks were delineated by the story in which they were contained. In the Greek theater, each person's tale was shaped and controlled by something that existed in a position of transcendence. The person's appropriate or inappropriate gesture towards this transcendent principle or deity not only immediately affected him, but impacted the lives of those around him—his family, clan, and city in the present *and* in the future. In short, the person and all related to him were understood as fated *because* of his relationship to the transcendent. He was responsible for fulfilling specific types of behavior—behavior that is in accord with each role he was called upon to play, be that the role of parent, child, beggar, king, warrior, or healer. By this process he was granted social significance. Society and the gods recognized him, identifying him by the signature of his acts, and the manner in which he moved about the stage and within the story assigned him. But this identification could only be granted if self-awareness were sacrificed to the role. In that event, the person's life was understood as archetypal because of the necessity of its inevitability. While all of these particulars regarding the person of Classical times essentially refer us to the Theater, to the accurate role-playing of a fictional person, the synonymous activities of the social-person limited by and obligated to social norms of behavior cannot avoid comparison.

Some would be tempted to find comfort in this theistic turn, to discover absolution in this connection between being and transcendence, expecting to find there a proximity to the Absolute. But in so doing they would fail to see that this formulation is just

---

[145]One need only cursorily examine the spate of autobiographies and book-length "interviews" during the past decade to discover that the original intent behind such texts, defense, is still very much alive.

that—a formulation by which it was *determined* that a self be arranged in such a manner. To interface with the world of social reality, of other actors bound to a common sense of being, one would have to identify himself with others and *to* others. This identification would not be simply a presenting of self, it would also have to signal where in the manifold levels of social reality "he" is to be located as a person. It was by not answering the defining lineaments of his assigned or chosen location that the *personae dramatis* of Greek tragedy suffered his due for such insubordination.

Nor should we overlook the fact that this paradigm for the person was selected from the machinery of the theater, the arena of Dionysos, which makes of him not simply the god of possession but specifically the god of possession by fiction, by the play of the characters that compose the drama. This god would possess us by locating us at stage-center, hidden and masked from others, prompting us to repeat our lines, to rehearse inevitabilities. It is only by this willingness repeatedly to move towards inevitability, the *necessitas* of the endless act to be re-enacted, that we fulfill the role of person. Of course, one must ask here what exactly is it that allows self-awareness to be moved towards such inevitabilities—to live within the limits of the idea of fatedness? In the past one would have ascribed it to a fear of God—but now we are forced to admit that it is more from a fear of our selves, of what we are told lies at the root of the person, a pre-ordained awareness, that bows us. It is here where the concept of the individual in the Western World bares its tableau of sufferings, that which immediately distinguishes it from other cultures and epoches: inherent and essential impurity. This is the reason why the story must be played out, act by act, line by line—the story is the vehicle of all hoped for purifications. Aristotle told us as much when he wrote that the drama enacted by masks in the theater is

> " . . . the imitation of an action that is serious and also, as having magnitude, complete in itself . . . with incidents arousing pity and fear, wherewith to accomplish its catharsis of such emotions."[146]

It is the self acting as a person that brings about catharsis, the cleansing of emotions, through the *imitation* of a serious and com-

---

[146]Aristotle, *Poetics*, vol. Two, para. 1449 25-28, p. 2320.

plete action of magnitude. The reason for the acting in the story is to assure one of catharsis, of a cleansing promised by the spiritual scripture scratched on the perennial body of the soul. For Socrates this cleansing was essential if we are to rid our souls of the evil they contain.[147] To this end only interrogation and confession can be called upon, thereby allowing the healer to teach the petitioner modesty by refuting and purging him of what are construed as prejudices until he is "made to think that he knows only what he knows, and no more."[148]

Here we have one of the many Platonic statements that mark the beginnings of psychotherapy, that impeach us to presume self-awareness itself contains an evil to be removed. To this end, Plato adds, the "purifier of soul" must approach the penitent as one who must be overcome, the healer's knowledge employed as a scourge upon his client's soul. In such a manner may the evil born of self-awareness be banished. And we are repeatedly told that this may be achieved only by the petitioner's obeisant discovery and acceptance within himself of a transcendent stuff sullied by his living. This is the function of the story, of his symptom, that he identify himself as sinner. Here, in this idea, do we find the source of all that we call pathology, its beginnings punctuated by Socrates' death wish.

What we have overlooked in the figure of Dionysos is that he was a god of appearances, the embodiment of the observation that all things *are* but appearance; that he was the personification of the affirmation of appearances, that things are but signs, and that the drama and tragedy played out on the stage commandeered by deities is the language of society.

---

[147]*Sophist*, 227d ff.
[148]*Ibid.*, 230c-d.

vi.

The Platonic and Aristotelian demand that the *polis* be self-sufficient eventually led to the concept of the person as independent and individual.[149] It is in the *Republic* where we are told that the city is the product of the mastery achieved by the domination of the inferior by the superior—the sober and self-mastered ruling those who are prisoners of "the mob of motley appetites and pleasures and pains one would find chiefly in children and women and slaves and in the base rabble of those who are free men in name."[150] Those who have simple and moderate appetites, aided by reason and right opinion, are few but will be found to be "the best born and the best educated."[151]

He then goes on to say that the city is composed of three natural types of people, each type fulfilling its function, and each corresponding with one of the three aspects of the human soul. From this it is apparent that the qualities composing the institutions of the city are to be found in the person as well, delineating his psyche.[152] We are told that one quality of the soul is that through which one learns, another through which one experiences anger, and a third through which the appetite for food, drink, love, and money, "the chief instrument for the gratification of such desires," is felt.[153]

As we can see from Plato's comments, there is a very intimate connection between the soul and the city, between the person and the events that occur within the gates of society. This should alert us to the problem in our tendency to isolate and locate specific types of expression within a special realm called the "psychopathological," thereby effectively lifting them out of those social

---

[149]Louis Dumont, "A modified view of our origins: the Christian beginnings of modern individualism," in Carrithers, Collins, Lukes, editors, *Category* . . . p. 96. Also see Plato's *Republic*, Book IV.

[150]*Republic*, 431b.

[151]*Ibid.*, 431c.

[152]*Ibid.*, IV, 435b-436a.

[153]*Ibid.*, 580d-581a.

sectors which seek to define themselves by their *absence*. There-fore, we should not only seek to differentiate pathologies (which are but negative-meanings needed to substantiate the integrity of a group's value), but rather the social structures that produce indices of exclusion in order to define themselves. The diagnostic differen-tiation of the excluded actually displays the types of social inter-actions a pathology is the product of. The symptom pantomimes the social setting that created the so-called pathology, the pathology itself being but a learned form of social response or protest.[154]

Early in the *Phaedrus*, Socrates states that it is only in the city where we may expect to gain knowledge.[155] We are to assume that knowledge is attainable there because it is only *there* where the human soul is actively engaged with each of its particulars. If this is so, then it is incumbent upon psychology, to the degree that it concerns itself with the soul, to seek the cause of pathology within the arena of the social, where persons interface with the world by their interaction with one another. To this end, it must seek to include the findings of sociology and cultural anthropology if it hopes to ever truly understand the dynamic operations of the psyche. The psyche, or consciousness, is not as much contained within us, as we are within it.

vii.

It was the responsibility of every Greek family to establish its own religion by choosing a deity or deities whose protection would be petitioned by reverence and sacrifice. While sacrifice to the family deity insured the immediate and future welfare of the family, its much more important function was the protection of its ancestors. The veneration and sacrifice offered up to the deity guaranteed that all of the family's ancestors would experience nothing but happiness and well-being in the afterlife. The possibil-ity of a family coming to an end was a great threat because the preceding generations that had given birth to it would suddenly and drastically suffer a reversal of their idyllic condition. It was for

[154]cf. Poncé, *Working*, pp. 160ff.
[155]*Phaedrus*, 230d.

82

this reason that marriage was obligatory, and celibacy (in some city states) considered a crime.[156]

Swanson has proposed that the phenomena of spirits (and by definition gods) in any culture refers us to "an organized cluster of purposes," maintained by specific groups "which persist over time and have distinctive purposes."[157] The one quality that distinguishes these groups is sovereignty:

> "A group has sovereignty to the extent that it has original and independent jurisdiction over some sphere of life—that its power to make decisions in this sphere is not delegated from outside but originates within it, and that its exercise of this power cannot legitimately be abrogated by another group. Although the term 'sovereignty' is commonly applied to nations or states, it can be applied to other groups as well."[158]

Furthermore, each institution has what Swanson refers to as its "constitutional structure," or reality frame by which it may be identified. The personification of these frames are what give rise to the image of deity.

Clearly, the initial formation of the city was dependent upon the consolidation and confederation of religious groups founded by prominent families. In ancient societies, as in the modern world, the family constituted a sovereign group or institution. But whereas in the world of Homer a man's prestige was bound up with his ancestry, alliance with other prominent persons (through marriage and friendship), and the politically astute distribution and application of his wealth, the establishment of the city removed political interaction from the arena of the family and redefined it as an issue of public interaction.[159] Obviously, the social processes by which the city came into existence were religious—

[156]cf., Fustel de Coulanges, *The Ancient City*, Garden City, New York: Doubleday & Company, Inc., n.d., p. 50. Much of the information contained in this paragraph may be found in this work.

[157]Guy E. Swanson, *The Birth of the Gods*, Ann Arbor, Michigan: The University of Michigan Press, 1968, pp. 18, 20.

[158]*Ibid.*, p. 20.

[159]cf., S. C. Humphreys, *Anthropology and the Greeks*, London, Boston, Melbourne and Henley: Routledge & Kegan Paul, 1978, p. 201.

and to the extent that these processes gave rise to the idea of the person, this concept also was religiously generated.[160]

The deities each city venerated were the personifications of its dominant groups. In much the same manner that the theriomorphic images of athletic teams in America are identified with a particular city, so too were the deities of ancient Greece the images of a city's power—and this power was the expression of the decisive roles the originating families held or lent themselves to in the city. Inevitably, "war or peace between two cities was war or peace between two religions."[161] When two cities fought against each other, the gods of those cities were believed to fight, and each man believed "he was fighting against the gods of another city."[162]

Little if anything has changed in this regard. War is still at base religious in nature. It is in fact the ultimate test of the religious superiority of one group over another, of the wrathful power that its deity is capable of distributing. It is this expression of power "in the name of the Father," that the patriot must embody if he is to develop the much touted heroic ego of depth psychology. It is within this frame of militaristic definitions that the concept of the norm in the Twentieth Century came into existence.

viii.

During the First World War the Division of Neurology and Psychiatry was created for the purpose of the administering of psychological tests to military personnel prior to their assignments.[163] The refinement of these tests occurred during World War

---

[160]cf. Thomas Luckmann, *The Invisible Religion*, London: The Macmillan Company, 1967, p. 49.

[161]Coulanges, *The Ancient City*, p. 209.

[162]*Ibid.*, p. 205.

[163]As Jung pointed out, it was the phenomenon of neuroses in World War I veterans with their seeming traumatic aetiology that "revived the whole question of trauma theory in neurosis." Jung, *CW*, vol. 16, para. 255. That is, if what we presently call "post-traumatic stress disorder" had not impressed itself upon the medical community, and if psychotherapy had not taken note of this social phenomena, we would more than likely not presently have a theory basing the aetiology of neurosis in trauma, and a therapy based upon it.

II under the direction of Dr. William Menninger, then Brigadier General of the Psychiatric Division of the Surgeon General's Office. It was Menninger who began the classification of mental illnesses that not only became the touchstone for diagnostic psychological procedures in all branches of the military at that time, but the matrix of the Diagnostic and Statistical Manual (DSM) of the American Psychiatric Association of the present. This introduction of psychiatric theory to the screening and selecting of military personnel eventually yielded a circumstance in which "more civilians were declared mentally unfit . . . more soldiers were classified as mentally ill, and more veterans now receive compensation of 'treatment' for mental illness than ever before in history,"[164] and on the other hand the claim of "unexpected success in the treatment of psychiatric patients."[165]

This latter claim, made at a time when thirty-seven per cent of all military medical discharges were for neuropsychiatric reasons (a quarter of the men withdrawn from combat zones), eventually led to the training of psychiatrists in on-the-spot diagnosis and treatment. The end result of this was that during the Korean conflict the withdrawal of soldiers from combat zones for neuropsychiatric reasons dropped to six percent overall, with the exception of the Marine Corp's more selective recruitment (or diagnostic) process yielding only a one per-cent withdrawal. All of this only gives justification to the observation that "the means of control in the military shifted from authoritarian techniques to more subtle, psychological manipulation."[166]

The psychological profile that would in time serve as the matrix for the concept of the norm demanded an individual who would respond unflinchingly, with little or no self-reflection regarding life-threatening situations, in the name of patriotism. This profile is already present in Plato when he calls for the establishment of a city state in which each citizen, from the cradle up, would be

---

[164]Thomas S. Szasz, M.D., *The Manufacture of Madness: A Comparative Study of the Inquisition and the Mental Health Movement*, New York: Harper & Row, 1970, p. 38.

[165]Paul Starr, *The Social Transformation of American Medicine*, New York: Basic Books, Inc., Publishers, 1982, p. 345.

[166]*Ibid.*, p. 344.

under the direct guidance of a commander. From this person one would learn when to bathe, eat, sleep, and keep watch, never thinking to perform an act that was not in accord with the community's needs.[167] The patriot of one culture is the terrorist of another—the two titles equally referring to a personality who either out of a sense of duty or faith is willing to sacrifice his life for his group: that is, a *pharmakon*.

The diagnostic manual created to meet military needs, by delineating the variety of styles that were not acceptable to the military and designating them as pathological, at the same time created the image of what is normal—by omission. Normality was generated out of the fields existing between pathological categories, found between the cracks of a socially created dimension called pathology which has come to serve as the yardstick of normality. Normality is simply what pathology is not (all of which is suspiciously reminiscent of the principle of the *Summum Bonum*, or "ultimate good," which informs us that evil is but the absence of the good). The matrix that served for the concept of the normal person in modern Twentieth Century America was militaristically determined. In other words, the ideal or normal image of the person pulsating at the base of Western diagnostic models is that of the patriot.[168]

War is not an instinct, a product of nature unalterable and inevitable (the brain-stem's threatening obstinacy), but society's defense of its own definition. That definition is carried by each of its members, and it is in the attempt and necessity of each of its members to fulfill their group's definition of the person that they are willing to die. What better proof that they are persons? Therefore, the extent to which a group insists upon the existence of an

---

[167]Plato, *Laws*, XII, 942a-e.

[168]The word "patriot" comes from the Greek pater (father), patrios (of one's fathers), and *patris*, (one's fatherland). There is no question that this term originally applied to the father's sons. The matrix of the patriot was the filial relationship and obligation of the son to the father. Mothers and daughters on the other hand celebrated the religion of their husbands and fathers, wives giving up their obligations to their fathers' religion when they married. The family, along with its worship, was patrilineal, and the son (according to Aeschylus) was the "savior of the paternal hearth." Coulanges, *The Ancient City*, p. 53.

a priori person is an indication of the willingness of that group to defend its definition to the point of waging war. Psychological statements and theorems are not the isolated and sophisticated indulgences most of us would prefer them to be; not either the product of solitary geniuses or rebellious upstarts, but the reflection of possibilities on their way towards (or arrived at) inevitabilities. They are the fulfillment of a group's justification. Nor need war be the mobilization of machined weapons and uniformed citizens: it is the spearhead of values militarized as moral and universal truths, their inevitable prejudices reasoned into a group's Commandments. Psychology should be about the business of asking itself (and others) how its occupation came about.

ix.

Plato, the father of all depth psychologies (sire of the Western psyche), informs us that the most sovereign portion of the soul resides in the head, its roundness mirroring the shape of the universe,[169] it actually being but the flower of the heavenly plant every human is. All of this is quite utilitarian in that the roots of this inverted plant are in heaven, which is what has brought the human body to its upright position.[170] So much for the divine portion of the soul.

As for the remaining two inferior portions, one is housed in the heart, the other in the liver.[171] That housed in the heart is the nobler and has been kept separate from the baser and impulsive portion by the division of "the cavity of the thorax into two parts, as the women's and men's apartments are divided in houses, the midriff . . . [serving as a] wall of partition between them."[172] Again, we are shown how much the city, its very architecture,

---

[169]*Timaeus*, 44d.

[170]*Ibid.*, 90a-b.

[171]*Ibid.*, 70a-b, 71b.

[172]*Ibid.*, 69e-70a. The typical house of the fifth Century B.C., when it could be afforded, contained separate rooms for slaves and women. The section containing these rooms were separated from the men's by a heavy door. cf. Bertha Carr Rider, Ancient Greek Houses, Chicago: Argonaut, Inc., 1964, p. 237.

becomes a model for the person. The social divisions of the sexes becomes the topology of the soul, causing not only the sexualization of the psyche to become its definition, but defining its composition in terms of opposition. This assignment of architectural constructs that sign the social positions of men and women in Greek culture, these visual and concrete statements announcing the social division of function between the sexes, become legitimatized by the Platonic story of the soul. The delineation and distribution of both power and knowledge among the sexes and the existing class system was rationalized by the divinity of story. This is yet another instance of how power on its way to becoming knowledge must first be storied. What was at first simply a social institution became immortalized as an archetype through the numinosity of story—for before the archetype can appear, the story must first be outlined. Plato not only sexualized the psyche, but placed it in opposition to itself as well. In this instance (and in others) he presents us with a paradigm that from that time until now has served to explain us to ourselves. What had been the product of a specific cultural milieu became the essential image of the psyche in the Twentieth Century.

The archetype is but the sign of the Institute that has legitimated itself through the story. It is for this reason that the proper study of the archetype should not proceed from the proposition that it is the matrix of events. To do so is to assign inevitability and constancy to social realities, and therefore to seek an archetypal and Providential justification for all inequities. The proper study of the archetype should proceed from the recognition of its social construction, and the understanding that the story it embodies is the diversionary technique by which the natural attitude is maintained. The numinosity of the story must be shed so that the surface of reality it conceals may be seen clearly for what it is.

Nor can one simply argue that social and physical reality is given its structure through the projection of the psyche's innate structure onto the world. One has to allow that the inverse is true: that the manner in which we order social reality becomes the model for the way we approach and structure the psyche. Plato's model of the psyche was an example of the way in which a culture justifies its position, whatever that position may be. It is, indeed, "held together by a mathematics-based *kosmos* or harmony, writ small in the individual psyche, larger in the well-ordered, consonant polis, largest in the harmony of the spheres that crowns the final book of *The Republic*."[173]

Such discriminations are social and immediate (of lived experience) and suggest the degree to which psychological structures are *created* by the needs of social reality. If a culture believes that the psyche is sexually compartmentalized, and that one of its compartments is inferior, then every member of that culture will more than likely *experience* their psyche as such and act in accord with the values that created the theory. The theory becomes an Institution which is then transmitted through the centuries, its autonomy giving us the sense of what we are told the presence of a god feels like.

As in the Egyptian instance, divinity again becomes embodied—for Plato's tripartite soul is dispersed and contained in the liver, heart, and brain. It is in the liver where the impulsive, hot-blooded, wanton and vainglorius, female portion of the soul resides. Its counterpart, heavenly, noble, moderate and male, is in the brain. Between these two is the mediating aspect of the soul located in the heart.[174]

X.

Freud's Trinitarian soul is not distributed amongst body organs as was Plato's, but is instead located within the parameters of the Cartesian mind-substance, a dimension clearly demarcated as something other than and residing outside of the dominion of matter and the body. Freud's Trinity is known as the Id, Ego, and Superego. The Id contains or represents the autonomous instinctual responses that seek to freely express themselves, answering Plato's liver-soul; the Superego is a form of social conscience that would disallow the Id's free expression, answering Plato's head-soul; and the Ego is that which stands between them determining which of the two to follow, always attempting to reconcile their conflictual intentions, answering Plato's heart-soul.

---

[173]Patrick Riley, *The General Will Before Rousseau*, Princeton: Princeton University Press, 1986, p. 257.

[174]*Phaedrus*, 253d-e.

The term Id was invented to translate the German *es*, which actually means "it"; Superego for "*Uber-Ich*," which in German means "Over-I," or "Upper-I" and is suggestive of "more than I," and Ego, *Ich*, which in German means "I."[175] In other words, Freud actually suggested that the self is composed of three distinct states: a state of otherness so divorced from consciousness, so undefinable and beyond subjectivity, that only the impersonal pronoun It could be used for its definition; another state that is both larger than and oversees the I, that while nonetheless being an integral division of the psyche, is more than the person, and actually in command of the person, the Over-I; and, finally, the I which by the definitions offered is sandwiched in between two aspects of its own being that are incomprehensibly larger and more powerful than itself. In other words, the person is here conceived as composed of two transcendent principles—the It and the over-I—that hem in the representative of self-awareness, the ego. One can't help but find a correspondence between Biblical Job and the predicament created for him by Yahweh and Satan.

Obviously existing between the two larger than self states of the It and the Over-I, the I is imaged as perpetually existing in the throes of conflict, always in danger of losing its limited autonomy to the hostility of one or the sovereignty of the other. The greater danger, we are told, is to be had in the subterranean It, where the energy lost to the I through repression must be discovered and returned to the I lest one be drained of all conscious volition. To regain this energy, the ego must access the forgotten origin of the conflict that caused the repression in the first place, its source often being the earliest conflict of childhood—when the I was apparently sufficiently present to discriminate what was conflictual and what not. Of course, a final resolution of the self's conflict can never be fully achieved by virtue of the fact that the It and Over-I will (by definition) always seek to gain supremacy. In essence, what we are told is that from the outset the self or the I finds itself torn between two opposing phenomena: Nature in the form of the instincts, and society in the form of the Superego, or over-I. At the very least, it is implied that the I can only gain a

---

[175]Bruno Bettelheim, *Freud and Man's Soul*, New York: Alfred A. Knopf, 1983, p. 59.

modicum of freedom by the retrieval of lost memories from the It.

Clearly, in Freudian theory, the idea is that the personal unconscious, with the aid of psychoanalysis, can eventually be emptied
of its repressed memories.[176] In this manner, the conflicts that
arose solely from repression, that lead to the Platonic contamina-
tion of the soul, may be resolved; but the immediately present and
the future promises to be rife with the conflicts generated by the
opposing wills of the Over-I and the It that the I will have to con-
tend with. This theoretical image of the person constructed by
Freud leaves little room for personal autonomy, and does little
more than suggest that the I is but a drunken boat tossed about
by desires and restrictions demonic in their demand for
subservience.

xi.

Jung's revision of this Freudian model of the person begins
with his observation that, in accordance with Freud's thesis,
dreams are but disguised repressions, and the phenomenon of
dreaming should end with the raising of all repressed contents up
from the It into the I. Noting that this was not the case, but that
the marked numinosity and imagery of dreams in such circumstances suggested a radical shift in content and direction, Jung
surmised that there was yet another unconscious—a collective
unconscious of universal composition and dynamic. The images
contained in this unconscious, he informs us, are of an impersonal
nature, constituting the typical patterns of actions and reactions
caused by the instincts. Here we must recall that the archetypes
were defined by him as the pictorial representations of the
instincts.[177] This in essence fulfilled Freud's statement that the
theory of the instincts was a new mythology, with a subtle twist:
in Jung, mythologies were understood as the stories created by the
interplay of the instincts, or the archetypes. He relocated the
image of the person even more squarely in Platonic theory (that
it is both mortal and divine) than Freud.

---

[176]Sigmund Freud, *The Interpretation of Dreams*, James Strachey, trans.
& ed., New York: Avon Books, 1965, p. 54.

[177]Jung, *CW*, vol. 8, para. 277.

Freud's position was that repression and conflict arise because of the interaction between parent and child—in the drama of archetypal fatedness given us in the mythical persons of Oedipus and Electra. Jung extended and deepened the conflict by not only finding its origin in personal and collective history, but by allowing all of the archetypal persons to access the self. Whereas Freud had limited himself to two archetypes by particularizing the soul's drive (libido) as sexual, Jung generalized the drive and by doing so prepared the foundation for a polytheistic definition of the instincts. This would then allow him to describe all psychological and social roles as having an *a priori* basis.

Freud had stated that the original and patricidal instinct had become a matter of genetics, and in that sense his vision was based upon an anthropological and Lamarckian imagination.[178] But in the final analysis his was a system of social dynamics, more in line with the issues that sociology tends to concern itself with. Jung, by creating the concept of the collective unconscious and the archetypes intuited that something more than genetics was operative in the transmission of patterns of action. We now know that the dynamism behind such transmission has to do with the phenomena of social institutions, and that the archetypal patterns he discerned are actually the type of social role-acting that these institutions promulgate and maintain from generation to generation. By speaking of institutional roles as archetypes, and proposing an *a priori* Platonic set of Ideas, the psychological person he proposed would have to be seen as influenced more by the past than the present. In this sense the person is every bit the Greek Classical person, a character possessed by a God.

Jung nowhere more clearly presents this idea than in his concept of the archetype of the self as "the organizer of the personality,"[179] "the archetype of order par excellence,"[180] and "the union of conscious (masculine) and unconscious (feminine)," adding to this the conclusion that the self's realization is equivalent to the

---

[178]Sigmund Freud, *Totem and Taboo*, James Strachey, trans. & ed., New York: W. W. Norton & Company, 1950, Chapter IV.

[179]Jung, *CW*, Vol. 10, para. 694.

[180]*Ibid.*, para. 805.

Westerner's arrival at monotheism as the natural development out of a more primitive or less differentiated polytheism.[181]

This latter judgement must, however, be revised in the light of recent and suggestive research: monotheism is "positively related to the presence of a hierarchy of three or more sovereign groups in a society," such as family/clan, city, empire; whereas polytheism, with its numerous deities, appears in "societies with social classes."[182] That is, neither monotheism nor polytheism is the result or reward of a developmental stage in consciousness. They are political positions. Each simply image, through the personification of their power, the manner by which social and political structures exemplifying rights are distributed. Any therapy, therefore, that defines itself within the context of either monotheism or polytheism—that bases the individuation of the person upon such theistic criteria—fulfills a function of socialization at the expense of self-knowledge. Such therapies would have to work, as a matter of course, from either a class-structure or hierarchical program of distinctions which presuppose what a "normal" person is. They would also inevitably seek to situate the individual within the strata appropriate to the group's expectations of his socially determined status. In either system, a successful therapy would be based upon the individual's fulfillment of or approximation with the concept of the ideal person. Such a self could be nothing more than a likely story.[183]

But Jung's most definitive statement regarding the archetype of the self and its role in psychology is to be found in the following:

> "The goal of psychological, as of biological, development is self-realization, or individuation. But since man knows himself only as an ego, and the self, as a totality, is indescribable and indistinguishable from a God-image, self-realization—to put it in religious or metaphysical terms—amounts to God's incarnation. That

---

[181]Jung, *CW*, vol. 5, paras. 147, 148; CW 9ii, paras. 426-427. In this latter work, the goal of psychological wholeness, the self, is equated with monotheism, whereas the anima/animus syzygy is equated with polytheism.

[182]Swanson, *The Birth of the Gods*, pp. 81, 96.

[183]Plato, *Statesman*, 268e-269.

is already expressed in the fact that Christ is the son of God. And because individuation is an heroic and often tragic task, the most difficult of all, it involves suffering, a passion of the ego: the ordinary, empirical man we once were is burdened with the fate of losing himself in a greater dimension and being robbed of his fancied freedom of will. He suffers, so to speak, from the violence done to him by the self. . . . The drama of the archetypal life of Christ describes in symbolic images the events in the conscious life—as well as in the life that transcends consciousness—of a man who has been transformed by a higher destiny."[184]

Here, clearly, we see that Jung's program aligns itself with the doctrinal demands of the Judeao-Christian tradition. The cultural specificity of this idea becomes embarrassingly apparent when we compare it with the Hindu image of the ideal person as one who has escaped *avidya*, ignorance, as the source of suffering.[185] From the perspective of this system suffering would be counter-productive and not transformative, and an indication of ignorance.

Thus, what Jung alerts us to is a social image of the Western and Christian person whose only road to salvation is the type of suffering the Freudian ego undergoes in the face of the It and the Over-I. By saying that the individual suffers by the "violence done to him by the self," Jung meant to stress that the process of individuation in the most positive sense of the term causes suffering. But if we look at this statement within the context of what we have said concerning the social construction of the idea of the person, we instead see that the violence done to the individual comes about because of the attempt to story him as the personification of an ideal, in this instance the archetype of the self—to turn him into an archetype. And by archetype, I remind you, what is meant is a socially created institution.

This procedure, which I shall address in Part III, is punctuated by the idea that a pre-existing principle of order, an ideal person, is given each of us in the archetype of the self if only we had a technique by which we could release or reach it. As it turns out,

---

[184]Jung, *CW*, vol. 11, para. 233.

[185]Cf. *The Yoga-System of Patanjali*, James Haughton Woods, trans., Cambridge: The Harvard University Press, 1927, Bk. II, 3, 24-26.

this technique is also present in the form of individuation—a process Jung informs us is constantly expressing itself at the unconscious level, awaiting its release up into the consciousness of the analyzed person.[186] This release or realization of the archetype of the self does not simply refer us to an alteration of consciousness, a change of attitude as it were, but

".... rather as the restoration of an original condition ... an ever-present archetype of wholeness which may easily disappear from the purview of consciousness or may never be perceived at all until a consciousness illuminated by conversion recognizes it in the figure of the Christ. As a result of this 'anamnesis' the original state of oneness with the God-image is restored. It brings about an integration, a bridging of the split in the personality caused by the instincts striving apart in different and mutually contradictory directions."[187]

In short, what Jung tells us is that there is an eternal and cosmic intelligence from which we are descended. In addition, we are to understand that Freud's super-ego or Over-I is nothing more than the archetype of the self in an unconscious and projected form,[188] and that the ego is but a relatively constant personification of the Self—a projection.[189] What we are being told is that the ego (that by which the individual subjectively experiences himself as being) must be supplanted by the collectivized image of what being is, and therefore must "be." In short, a true consciousness is an approximation of the archetype of the self[190] which can only be

---

[186]Jung, *CW*, vol. 7, para. 186; vol. 11, para. 756.

[187]Jung, *CW*, vol. 9ii, para. 73. Jung is here discussing the damaged and corrupted God-image in humans and the problem of its restoration outlined in St. Augustine's *De Trinitate*, XIV, 22 as exemplary of his own formulation of the archetype of the self and the individuation process.

[188]Jung, *CW*, vol. 11, para. 396.

[189]Jung, *CW*, vol. 14, para. 129. This statement must be taken in conjunction with Jung's position that the Spirit Mercurius in alchemy refers us to the unconscious (in both its subjective and collective form, cf. CW, 14, paras. 117, 660, 700), and is in addition an image of the archetype of the self. *Ibid*, para. 717.

[190]Jung, *CW*, vol. 11, para. 401.

brought about by the abolishment of egohood[191] in favor of the socialized self. What all of this suggests is that the process of individuation (not to mention the psychoanalytical process of Freud), in that it seeks to inaugurate a self modeled along Judeao-Christian definitions of the person, actually displays a technique by which such a norm is guaranteed.

But what is the mechanism by which such a therapeutic transfiguration of the person comes to pass?

---

[191]"The [psychotherapeutic] goal is transformation—not one that is predetermined, but rather an indeterminable change, the only criterion of which is the disappearance of egohood." *Ibid.*, para. 904; also see CW 14, para. 778: ". . . *the experience of the self is always a defeat for the ego.*" Jung's italics.

Part III

Transfigurations

"... and even the religious and political fundamentalism that was breaking out or persisting wherever one looked was an indication that many, indeed most, people could not stand themselves if they were not observed by someone, and would flee either into the fantasy of a personal god or into an equally metaphysically conceived political party that (or who) would observe them ..."

Friedrich Durrenmatt, *The Assignment*

"But is he really a physician, this ascetic priest? ... He combats only suffering itself, the discomfiture of the sufferer, not its cause, not the real sickness: this must be our most fundamental objection to priestly medication."

Friedrich Nietzsche, *On the Genealogy of Morals*

"(Come in under the shadow of this red rock)
... I will show you fear in a handful of dust."

T. S. Eliot, *The Waste Land*

i.

Most sociologists and cultural anthropologists agree that in the final analysis psychotherapy is a socialization technique by which an identified or elected deviant population is either converted to the norm, or secluded and maintained by the norm. As cultural anthropologists have observed, the cooperative decision-making or negotiations of a patient in ritual-healing situations appears in a number of cultures around the world. The role of "patient" in both primitive and modern cultures is learned through dissemination of the role's requirements through the type of seepage normal enculturation incurs. In our culture the delineation of the role (as well as that of many other roles) is given us through the communication mediums of television, movies, drama, literature, and the images offered us by advertising. In primitive cultures the role is either revealed by those who have been patients, or by the depiction of the ill-person in the stories of their mythology. Persons in both types of cultures who feel they are socially out of context and wish to be included in the norm must first be converted to an assigned symptom via what the English psychoanalyst Michael Balint has described as the "apostolic function" of the doctor

> "—suggesting that the doctor has definite ideas as to how patients ought to behave when ill and that he subtly induces (or 'converts') each patient to have the kind of illness he considers appropriate to the situation."[192]

All of this only punctuates the observation that "psychological theories . . . serve to legitimate the identity-maintenance and identity-repair procedures established in society, providing the theoret-

---

[192]Edwin M. Schur, *Labeling Deviant Behavior*, New York: Harper & Row Publishers, 1971, p. 61.

ical linkage between identity and world, as these are both socially defined and subjectively appropriated."[193] This "conversion" to a symptom is achieved through an interpretation of those selected portions of a person's history that can be best aligned with a codified system of diagnostic profiles—profiles which every modern practitioner would agree are malleable in that no one individual could ever either fully meet the exact criteria of a specific profile, or be thought to be without features not included in that profile. The role of the patient in the Zar cult of Ethiopia is a case in point.

The Zar cult deals with zar-spirit-possession, the symptoms of which include "proneness to accidents, sterility, convulsive seizures, and extreme apathy."[194] The procedure that follows is known by everyone in the culture, whether they have been a patient or not:

> "The doctor will lure his own zar into possessing him in a trance, and through his intercession try to lure the unknown zar of the patient ('his horse') into public possession. Then the spirit will be led to reveal his identity by means of adroit cajolery, promises, and threats. . . . The demands of the zar will be negotiated through a lengthy process of financial dickering. Finally, the patient will be enrolled, for the rest of his life, in the 'zar society' of fellow-sufferers, renting, as it were, his temporary freedom from relapse through regular donations and by means of participation in the worship of the spirit. . . . The chronic patient finds many benefits as a member of the zar society. *He calls attention to himself as an individual and may rise in social status in the family or community.*"[195]

Clearly, there are many comparisons between this procedure and those presently employed in modern Western psychotherapy.

The conversion to first symptom and then cure is brought about by an agency common to both primitive and modern

---

[193]Peter L. Berger & Thomas Luckman, *The Social Construction of Reality*, New York: Doubleday, 1967, p. 176.

[194]Simon D. Messing, "Group Therapy and Social Status in the Zar Cult of Ethopia," in *Magic, Witchcraft, and Curing*, John Middleton, editor, New York: The Natural History Press, 1967, p. 285.

[195]*Ibid.*, pp. 285-286. My emphasis.

therapeutic institutions: the story. In primitive cultures the greater portion of the shaman's therapeutic tools are the stories composing his group's mythology. His differential diagnosis is essentially achieved by the selection of some feature of that mythology which at one and the same time explains the origin of a specific disorder as well as the prescribed cure.[196]

Lévi-Strauss points out that by providing the patient with a story, the patient is given

"a *language* by means of which unexpressed, and otherwise inex-pressible, psychic states can be immediately expressed. And it is the transition to this verbal expression—at the same time making it possible to undergo in an ordered and intelligible form a real experience that would otherwise be chaotic and inexpressible—which induces the release of the physiological process, that is, the reorganization, in a favorable direction, of the process to which the sick . . . [person] is subjected . . . .as this experience becomes structured [by the story], regulatory mechanisms beyond the subject's control are spontaneously set in motion and lead to an orderly functioning."[197]

Of course it is assumed here that the regulatory functions that lead to a "cure" need to be socially ordered. If psychic disorders come about because of "bad" or failed stories and are corrected by "good" stories (i.e., collectively approved meanings), would it necessarily follow that "no stories" would yield no results? Rather, we must ask ourselves, how can we be certain that the stories themselves have not generated validating psychological structures based upon dichotomous and conflictual values *that caused specific disorders and their panaceas to occur in the first place?*

An equivalent procedure occurs in modern psychotherapy in that the theoretical canon of the school the therapist had been initiated and trained in constitutes his mythology. Freud was well aware of this when he wrote that, "The theory of the instincts is

---

[196]A good and detailed analysis of the transposition of story to therapeutic-ritual can be found in Mary C. Wheelwright, *Hail Chant and Water Chant*, Santa Fe: Museum of Navaho Ceremonial Art, 1946.

[197]Claude Levi-Strauss, *Structural Anthropology*, New York: Anchor Books, 1967, pp. 192, 194. His emphasis.

so to say our mythology. Instincts are mythical entities, magnificent in their indefiniteness."[198]

The recent mythologizing of lives suggested by the plethora of publications purporting to be revelatory and therapeutic in nature reveals the extent to which such mythological styles have become an essential part of the fabric of the natural attitude in the Twentieth Century. By them we are told that both our pathologies and our cures are to be found in the gods and goddesses of ancient cultures—that, in short, one's destiny must be petitioned for. But petitioned for to whom?

Whereas in a primitive culture the patient's complaint is structured and storied by an existing and consistent collective mythologem, the petitioner of modern psychotherapy may (to all appearances[199]) chose his mythology, i.e., the therapeutic school he imagines best corresponds to his needs. That a wide variety of therapeutic schools of differing philosophical orientation claim cures should indicate that it is not the technique of any one school that is more efficacious than another. If the goals of psychotherapy are in general the socialization and normalization of the individual along the lines of a culture-specific natural attitude—if all roads lead to Rome—the philosophic or political position of each school are ultimately in agreement with one another. In addition, the search for the "right" therapist informs us that the petitioner already "knows" something about what and who will cure him. He is in essence seeking a therapist with an image, attitude, and technique congruent with his need to be storied in a specific manner. Of course, this selective process is a two-way street in that

> "Like the shaman, the psychoanalyst maximizes the likelihood of success by his selection of cases for treatment . . . the psychotherapist's personal predilections may influence his choice of patients and his relative success with different types. Recognizing this, some psychiatrists will not attempt to treat

---

[198]Sigmund Freud, *New Introductory Lectures on Psychoanalysis*, James Strachey, trans. & ed., New York: W.W. Norton & Co., 1965, p. 95.

[199]In that all of the major depth psychologies are based upon an essentially Idealistic perspective regarding the nature of normalcy and the social-construction of the person, the idea of choice is self-illusory.

alcoholics, while others avoid hysterics; some believe they do especially well with depressed patients, others regard their forte as schizophrenics."[200]

Whereas the technique or philosophical perspective of the practitioner may or may not be initially known by the petitioner, the attitude of the practitioner is very much a part of the image that the petitioner carries with him regarding what the "right" doctor or healer should be like. This situation is obviously in direct contrast to pre-literate societies where the "shaman represents and transmits the unified, all-encompassing world view of his society,"[201] thereby offering the primitive petitioner seemingly little choice in the selection of therapeutic styles. Choice in modern societies occurs precisely because there no longer *appears* to exist an all-encompassing world view or metaphysic manageable enough for one group to sustain and promulgate. Any number of factors ranging from social class, race, religion, socio-economic accessibility, education, etc., go into determining the image of the "right" therapist.

In short, the petitioner's search is for an individual who best corresponds to the collectivized image of "healer" or "doctor," and who responds to the petitioned for unfolding of this image. It is the reciprocal reception on the part of both parties of unfoldings regarding the appropriateness of the image of doctor and patient that signals the beginning of psychotherapy. All of this is to say is that projection is not as unconscious a procedure as most make it out to be, for one has to "also keep in mind the psychological fact that there is always a 'hook' for every projection."[202] The therapist who receives the projection does so because he or she in some manner either embodies the qualities of the petitioner's internalized image of what will heal him, or believes he can effectively fulfill them. It therefore appears that what we have in the act of projection is actually a contractual agreement between two or

---

[200]Jerome D. Frank, *Persuasion and Healing: A Comparative Study of Psychotherapy*, New York: Schocken Books, 1974, pp. 173, 184.

[201]*Ibid.*, p. 179.

[202]Marie-Louise von Franz, *Projection and Re-Collection in Jungian Psychology*, La Salle & London: Open Court, 1980, p. 26.

more people. In other words, the term "projection" within the arena of a therapeutic encounter actually refers us to a conscious, though often unverbalized, agreement. It would therefore be more appropriate to speak of psychic congruence than projection in that both parties are cooperating with one another. It is this psychic congruence that then allows the special case of projection, the transference, to satisfy itself. In turn, the therapist essentially complies with the petitioner's request to play out the role of an agent of social control, which is "merely a formalization and elaboration of similar efforts at maintaining consistency through biographical reconstruction that all of us engage in continually in our everyday interactions."[203]

It is at this juncture where, as we mentioned earlier, the apostolic function of the therapist comes into full play and negotiations regarding the nature of the symptom and its assessment within the boundaries of the therapist's mythology begin. It is to this end that the petitioner as patient supplies, or has ferreted out of him, the life history that will become both his symptom and his story. What in effect occurs at this point is an elegant shifting of biographical material in an effort to "discover" the underlying causes of the presenting symptom on the one hand, and the creation of a diagnosis on the other. In other words, biographical material must be found or created that will "fit" within the diagnostic categories of the therapist's mythology. It is in this manner that the symptom becomes legitimated and meaningful.

John Lofland, in reviewing the story of mass murderer Charles Whitman (who in 1966, from a tower at the University of Texas, shot fourteen people), discussed how necessary the biographical reconstruction of a life along deviant lines is in legitimatizing a psychological assessment. In Whitman's case no previous history of either deviant or pathological behavior could be found, thus leading Lofland to conclude:

> "The problem posed in the effort to reconstruct consistently Whitman's biography possibly explains the later popularity of attributing his acts to an alleged brain tumor. When social and psychological explanations fail, one can always try biological or

---

[203]Schur, *Labeling*, p. 55.

physiological ones. Regardless of the character of the account, Actor must be accounted for . . . we see [here] most clearly the social need of Others to render Actors as consistent objects . . . [and that] there must be a special history that specially explains current imputed identity. Relative to deviance, the present evil of current character must be related to past evil that can be discovered in biography."[204]

Erving Goffman has in turn pointed out that the true purpose behind case records in mental institutions (and therefore the biography of a therapist's patient in private practice) is to

"show the ways in which the patient is sick and the reasons why it was right to commit him [i.e., to take the petitioner on as patient] and is right currently to keep him committed [i.e., to keep him in therapy], and this is done by extracting from him his whole life course a list of those incidents that have or might have had 'symptomatic' significance."[205]

Thus, the construction of the case history is such that the therapist seeks to legitimatize the petitioner's deepest fears about himself—that there is not just something presently wrong with him, but that there has *always* been something wrong with him. That the petitioner/patient can accept this idea at all has to do with the fact that the Western World is at base a guilt culture: "A society that inculcates absolute standards of morality and relies on men's developing a conscience is a guilt culture by definition . . . [guilt cultures rely] on an internalized conviction of sin."[206]

Here we also more than likely have the source of the Freudian (and now general) concept of self-deception assumed operating behind the mechanisms of defense. This paradoxical condition

---

[204]John Lofland, *Deviance and Identity*, Englewood Cliffs, New Jersey: Prentice-Hall, 1966, pp. 150, 151.

[205]Erving Goffman, *Asylums*, Garden City, N.Y.: Doubleday Anchor, 1961, pp. 155-6.

[206]Ruth Benedict, *The Chrysanthemum and the Sword*, New York: New American Library, 1974, pp. 222-3. Freud only punctuates the matter when he writes, "The earliest moral precepts and restrictions in primitive society have been explained by us as reactions to a deed which gave those who performed it the concept of 'crime' . . . *This creative sense of guilt still persists among us.*" Freud, *Totem and Taboo*, p. 159. My emphasis.

which by definition states that an individual can at one and the same time be conscious and unconscious of either a desire, impulse, need, or understanding is based upon our culture-specific belief that the psyche is inherently divided and divisive—one portion of it subject to "other" forces, be those forces God, the devil, spirits, or the unconscious.[207] One need go no further than the closing sentence of the Lord's Prayer to discover the degree to which the Western psyche has been ransomed into a daily petitioning for safe journey through the passage of a day: "And lead us not into temptation, but deliver us from evil."[208] According to this, it is God Himself that leads us into the very temptations that give rise to yet further experiences in guilt. The matter is no different in the *Book of Job* where we discover Yahweh entering into a wager with Satan concerning the stalwartness of a true believer in God. It is Yahweh himself who heaps the many injustices on the shoulders of Job in an attempt to force him into temptation. It is in such a manner that the Westerner may at one and the same time be held blameless for actions which he at the same time is held legally responsible for. There is very little difference between the religious defense of possession and the Twentieth-Century legal defense of the insanity plea.

The ascription of self-deception by religious authority has now passed into the hands of the therapist who by a series of therapeutic interpretations based upon ostensibly moralistic judgements—resistance, blocking, splitting, denial, all terms stressing the existence of deception on the part of the patient—allows the therapist in his position of social authority to convince the patient that he is incapable of trusting himself. This fulfills the Platonic job-

---

[207]Nor can this devilish state of affairs be reconciled by attributing to paradox a "higher level of intellect" which protects us from hybris. (Jung, *CW* 11, para. 417.) To attribute to contradiction a form of intelligence, inspired or otherwise, can only serve to maintain the ignorance that the natural attitude is dependent upon for its maintenance. The paradoxes presented us in both religion and psychology simply reflect the willingness of common sense to nurture the numinosity that inevitably accompanies ignorance. What is truly hybristic is the position that such a state of affairs is divinely sanctioned.

[208]*Matthew* 7:13.

description of the therapist I referred to earlier, and which is worth repeating in full:

> "So the purifier of the soul is conscious that his patient will receive no benefit from the application of knowledge until he is refuted, and from refutation learns modesty; he must be purged of his prejudices first and made to think that he knows only what he knows, and no more."[209]

Clearly, the patient's "prejudices" are his own understanding of what is going on, and the one who must be seen as knowing more then he must be the therapist. But the fulcrum of this passage is the statement that the patient, if he is to be at all served in this setting, must be brought to a position of modesty. This latter demand seems innocuous enough until we discover that to Plato's way of thinking modesty is a form of fear, and by implication fearlessness a form of impudence.

> "And consequently each of us needs to be at once free from fear and filled with fear . . . And when we intend to make a man immune from various fears, we achieve our purpose by bringing him into contact with fear, under the direction of the law."[210]

That is, whether the law be that of the courts or of the therapeutic encounter, the unruly and impassioned aspect of the soul—that which gives rise to a "bad reputation from some unworthy act or speech"—must be brought to the fear in modesty by the fear of public censure.[211] It is only in this manner that "at long last the soul of the lover follows after the beloved with reverence and awe,"[212] which is an apt description of the transference that Freud and much of psychotherapy demands if it is to be effective.[213]

---

[209]*Sophist*, 230c-d.

[210]*Laws* I: 647b-c.

[211]*Laws* I:647a.

[212]*Phaedrus* 254e.

[213]"If the theory of analytic technique is gone into, it becomes evident that transference is an inevitable necessity . . . Practical experience . . . shows conclusively that there is no means of avoiding it." Sigmund Freud, "Fragment of an Analysis of a Case of Hysteria," in *Collected Papers*, New York: Basic Books, 1959, Vol. 3, p. 139. It is to Jung's credit that he stressed such a demand as untenable, and the transference more of a hindrance than an aid. cf. Jung, *CW*, vol. 16, para. 359.

To reiterate: in all likelihood, the phenomenon of self-deception as a defining characteristic of the Western psyche complements the needs of a guilt-culture to maintain the idea of sin as the essence of the person. The ascription of self-deception to an individual or individuals by another individual or institution demands that the latter be in a position of power and authority. Of all of the psychotherapeutic theories, this is the most powerful and most damning in that it can and has been too readily employed to undermine the judgement of the client.

ii.

That the construction of the symptom can coalesce around a socialized sense of guilt lies at the heart of all present therapies. For therapy to "work" the therapist himself must not only be in full agreement with the idea of an original sin (in whatever metaphoric form its parameters have been storied), but must also believe that he is capable of absolving the petitioner of his guilt *and* his unconscious behavior. This, as I have shown above, is possible because of the West's belief that an original self has been impeded by the experience of one's humanity.

However, a cursory observation of the site at which what is deemed pathological behavior occurs reveals that the performing individual is actively engaged with the environment, that his faculties are operative (pro or con of whether or not someone else deems them deficient), and that his presence *demands* response. To label such an actor "unconscious" of his behavior is to presume that pathological activity is without intention. Whether or not one agrees or sympathizes with the events occurring at the site is not the issue. What is the issue is the *fact* of the engagement—that a non-linguistic conversation is underway. The performing individual is stating that he is acting in a pathological manner. That any number of cultural anthropologists have noted certain types of aberrant behavior are peculiar to one group of people and no other, suggests that one must first know what is considered pathological in order to act in such a recognizable manner. There is consciousness here. We may only legitimately suggest that "consciousness" as we define it—as the essence of "normal" behavior—is absent if the activity has been brought about by organic phenomena that override conscious volition.

That the consciousness of the "pathologically" performing individual defies and disrupts a socially defined reality frame is not enough reason to deem it "unconscious." It is indeed a disguised act, one through which the individual makes a statement. The fact that such pathologies remain consistent, elegant if you will, indicates that we are present to a language. The same thing is being "said" over and over again. Again, it may not be a language that we like experiencing, but it is a language in that its presentation is identifiable, a signature of the personality by which you locate him within the context of a specific type of socially defined behavior. The person so behaving presents himself to you as a statement, as an aside he feels (or has been taught) he may only express himself through. What makes the statement pathological is an assumed response on the part of the viewer. That is why the actor "speaks" in such a manner. Such conversations occur in a field of social consciousness shared by the performer and any others who may be within his vicinity. The actor acts and is therefore (at the very least) peripherally aware of his acts even as he is "unconsciously" performing them. That the actor performs such "symptoms" in the actual field of his consciousness, indicates that they are there for him and with him. They are conscious acts, gestures that do communicate meaning to a recipient—and here I do not mean the "trained" recipient, the psychotherapist, but the average person, who in turn reacts to them in a manner socially guaranteed by the actor's gesture.

Anthropology reports that individuals who present themselves for initiation into trance and non-trance possession cults must produce and display psychological and/or physiological phenomena that the cult requires as prerequisites for admission, and as proof of completion (inclusion) for full promotion. Thus, symptoms in these situations are a form of compliance to the processes that allow full inclusion in the perspectives (in this instance trance/non-trance possession forms of consciousness) they delineate. All psychotherapeutic training programs follow this model.[214] This ability of the individual to conform to a perspective

---

[214]"The training analysis . . . is not complete until the candidate produces memories, thoughts, and feelings in a form that confirms the doctrines of the institute." Jerome D. Frank, *Persuasion*, p. 172.

by producing symptomatology thought to be autonomous and beyond control is, I strongly suggest, indicative of the degree to which psychological symptomatology is consciously produced. Here I am not attributing willful and purposeful deceptiveness to individuals producing such symptomatology, but rather indicating that pathological symptomatology is indicative of a particular form of resistance disguised or storied in the shape of a socially formed compliance. In that sense all such symptomatology is archetypal; what we are witness to is the venting process of Institutions rather than the aberration of individuals.[215] The humorous observation that individuals are capable of producing Freudian dreams in Freudian therapy, and Jungian dreams in Jungian therapy therefore has little to do with the differences in process these therapies claim bring about such therapeutic phenomena.[216] The different expressions of "development," "transformation," and "resolution" are a direct product of the individual's alignment with a perspective and the resultant expression of a "process" that must be successfully displayed before one might be thought of as "cured," or in the case of the student-therapist, "trained."

iii.

All of this is to punctuate that biographical reconstruction (whether it be found in Freud, Jung, or any of the branches of their schools) is nothing more than the sophisticated elaboration of primitive styles of healing—a new shamanism. The value in discovering the historical continuity of this therapeutic principle (aside from revealing that the phrase "modern psychological

---

[215]cf. Lenora Greenbaum, "Possession Trance in Sub-Saharan Africa: A Descriptive Analysis of Fourteen Societies," in Erika Bourguignon, editor, *Religion, Altered States of Consciousness, and Social Change*, Columbus, Ohio: Ohio State University Press, 1973, pp. 58-87.

[216]Jung explained why he thought this was indeed the case when he wrote, "There are people who can read my books and never have a dream of anything reminiscent of my writings, but it is true that if you understand what you have read, you get a frame of mind or a problematical outlook which you did not have before, and that, of course, influences your dreams." C. G. Jung, *Letters*, Princeton: Princeton University Press, 1975, Vol. 2, p. 187.

theory" is a misnomer) is that it explains why so much of depth psychology has appropriated the trappings of religion and not philosophy. And here I do not mean to be facetious in suggesting that psychotherapy presently thinks of itself and operates as a religion. The most recent call to such religious conversion has been succinctly mapped out by a modern-day Jungian therapist:

> "We would examine psychological observations through religious positions: which God is at work. Here we are opening into the 'religion of psychology' by suggesting that psychology is a variety of religious experience.
>
> Psychology as religion implies imagining all psychological events as effects of Gods in the soul, and all activities to do with soul, such as therapy, to be operations of ritual in relation to the Gods. Our theories about the soul are then also myths, and the history of depth psychology a kind of Church history . . . and above all, depth psychology's impetus to salvation. . . . Ultimately we shall admit that archetypal psychology is theophanic: personifying, pathologizing, psychologizing, and dehumanizing are the modes of polytheizing, the means of revealing Gods in a pluralistic universe."[217]

If psychology is nothing more than a religion dressed in medical smock, then its pronouncements and theories must be taken as matters of faith—as the abstracts of Ecclesiastical councils posing as Psychological Congresses. Where then once we tithed yearly, now we do so weekly, and on an hourly basis to priests neutered in the service of another Mother church. And what good would yet another faith further us after several thousand years of the disavowal of evil by faiths that have themselves furthered the spread of prejudice, intolerance, and superstition under banners of war held up in the name of peace? What business has psychology—which promised to bring us to awareness—with the adoration and petitioning of power in the guise of deities, and how long should we wait for their compassion *this time*? How could religion as psychology be any different, and what would be changed but the name of power?

---

[217]James Hillman, *Re-Visioning Psychology*, New York: Harper & Row, 1975, pp. 227-8.

It is important we remember that the Asclepian cult of healing appeared at a time when Greek religion began to lose its impact and hold in its own culture. All of this is in accord with the observation that "when *previous or traditional forms of social control are seen as inefficient or unacceptable*, it is likely that medical controls will appear."[218] It is also important to take note of the fact that once this cult became established as a medical institution, it then rapidly developed into a religious cult.[219] One could say that the recent developments in depth psychology that cause it to concern itself with the issues of psyche as spiritual realities are the first indications of a movement towards a new religio-medical cult, a cult of psyche. This call to heal psyche within the envelope of a metaphysic or religion serves an established healing profession in its historically traditional move towards its inauguration as a religious cult, and in time into a collective religion.

Furthermore, Jung's observations regarding the "transference relationship" created by both therapy and religious confession, along with the fact that in such transference the Church, priest, and therapist replace the parents, "and to that extent . . . free the individual from the bonds of the family,"[220] punctuates the degree to which the function of psychology has become that of religion. Jung admits that the religious institution of confession was created for the purposes of socialization, stressing that it was the psychotherapeutic transference to the priest that allowed him to become "the responsible leader of his community."[221] Modern man, he adds, ideally does not (or should not) want to be led, but rather seeks to stand on his own feet. It is for this reason that the major role of the therapist, in contrast to the priest, is one of analyzing the transference which essentially the priest passively

---

[218]Peter Conrad, "On the Medicalization of Deviance and Social Control," in *Critical Psychiatry*, David Ingleby, editor, New York: Pantheon Books, 1980, p. 112. Conrad's emphasis.

[219]Emma Edelstein and Ludwig Edelstein, *Asclepius: A Collection and Interpretation of the Testimonies*, Baltimore, Md.: The Johns Hopkins Press, 1945, pp. 67ff.

[220]Jung, *CW*, vol. 4, para. 434.

[221]*Ibid.*, para. 433.

received and lived out.[222] By these observations Jung means to imply that the therapist and therapy have moved a step beyond the role and function of the priest and Church. However as long as therapy's fulcrum point is the confessional, what has really transpired is the development of a new priestly role (as Hillman stresses) and not the demarcation of a new and secular role called therapist. The Confessional was and still is but a concealed form of interrogation. The concept of the person as penitent/client rests upon the idea of a sinful or maladapted soul—upon moral issues that are at times construed as inherent and innate, which in point of fact are simply failures, inabilities, or refusals to comply with social directives. In addition, the individual who is attended to as client must first admit (i.e., agree with doctrinal issues concerning the nature of the soul) that his greatest sin has been one of sinning against himself. Therefore, true wholeness or completion may only be acquired by a continuing posture of self-abnegation in relationship to one's self. Religious mortification has become supplanted by interminable analysis.

Foucault, in his tracing of the methods by which society creates and manages behavioral conformity, demarcating areas of human life into the regulated and the unregulated, controlled and uncontrolled, in one work discusses the degree to which Christian spiritual practices helped create the modern concept of the self with the technique of self-revelation, or confession:

> ". . . in the Christianity of the first centuries, there are two forms of disclosing self, of showing the truth about oneself. The first is *exomologesis*, or a dramatic expression of the situation of the penitent as sinner which makes manifest his status as sinner. The second is what was called in the spiritual literature *exagoreusis*. This is an analytical and continual verbalization of thoughts carried on in the relation of complete obedience to someone else. This relation is modeled on the renunciation of one's own will and of one's own self."[223]

---

[222]*Ibid.*, para. 435.

[223]Michel Foucault, "Technologies of the Self, in *Technologies of the Self,* Luther H. Martin, Huck Gutman, Patrick H. Hutton, editors, Amherst, Mass.: University of Massachusetts Press, 1988, p. 48.

As Jung himself (as well as others who have since followed him) indicated, there is little difference between the priest-petitioner/patient-therapist syzygies in modern psychotherapy. The petitioner must appropriately present himself as a patient and follow clear rules regarding how he is to maintain his patienthood, the most stringent and necessary rule being the verbalization of inner thoughts as indicative of the legitimacy of his role as patient. This "Christian hermeneutics of the self with its deciphering of inner thoughts . . . implies that there is something hidden in ourselves and that we are always in a self-illusion which hides the secret."[224]

Of course, one would argue here that the modern Western World, and American psychology in particular, is far removed from the effect of religious doctrinal teachings; that the sophistication, urbanization, and education of the Westerner (not to mention his discreet disavowal of religion in his everyday life) leaves no room for the proliferation of the moralizing techniques of the Judeao-Christian tradition. However, as Foucault also points out, whereas it is true that the ecclesiastical institutionalization of pastoral power came to an effective close sometime during the Eighteenth Century, its function did not. That is, "a new distribution, a new organization of this kind of individualizing power" occurred which shifted the focus of salvation in the next world to the focus of salvation in this world through the institutionalization of a series of powers whose ethics were originally given birth to by ecclesiastical thought in the first place: "those of the family, medicine, psychiatry, education, and employers."[225] It was in such a manner that the secret of self that has to be revealed through the confessional has maintained itself into the twentieth Century as a psychological concern. The way to the secret, obviously, is through verbalization of our history so that the reconstructive process of biography-management might "return" us, or at the very least, bring us to a self that is in accord with *others*, but not necessarily with oneself:

---

[224]*Ibid.*, p. 46.

[225]Hubert L. Dreyfus & Paul Rabinow, *Michel Foucault: Beyond Structuralism and Hermeneutics*, Chicago: The University of Chicago Press, 1983, second edition, pp. 214, 215.

"Through confession I throw myself *into the arms of humanity again*, freed at last from the burden of moral exile. The goal of the cathartic method is full confession—not merely the intellectual recognition of the facts with the head, but their confirmation by the heart and the actual release of suppressed emotion." [226]

But inasmuch as the process becomes metamorphisized into a story, it becomes fictionalized and therefore represents a fabricated reality. That is, the individual's existence becomes defined by the mythology or cosmology of the culture his therapist feels is appropriate to his condition. In this regard, the therapist is in a position of assigning his patient to a reality (or a reality to his patient) that he believes is an appropriate container. Such an instance is given us in the therapeutic encounter of a therapist with a woman who had spent years dealing with psychotic episodes. We are told that he felt it was her story that, "had to be doctored, not her: it needed reimagining. So I put her years of wastage into another fiction." [227] In other words, she was given a fiction to live in, a "better" story— the move discussed in the pages above as a form of biographical reconstruction psychotherapy has taken upon itself to perform.

But we should not lose sight of the fact that as the patient-petitioner follows the structured course of the primitive patient, so too does the therapist follow the guidelines of the shaman. As the shaman turns to the divine past contained in story, so the therapist turns to the secular past to create a fiction—the origins of the symptom. The therapist, as he presently practices, is enticed by the client's memory of his past, believing that it is there where things will be understood. And here I refer to the past as defined in therapy: as a beginning point, as the origin of the client's delusions and illusions, the *prima materia* of the supposed *pharmakon* or therapeutic medicine, the origin of the person turned client. Thus a lot of time is spent remembering the past, going over the past, discussing the past, and analyzing the past. It is believed that

---

[226]Jung, *CW*, vol. 16, para. 134. My emphasis. Also, "The first beginnings of all analytical treatment of the soul are to be found in its prototype, the confessional." Jung *CW*, vol. 16, para. 123.

[227]James Hillman, *Healing Fiction*, Barrytown, New York: Station Hill, 1983, p. 17.

through understanding the past the present shall become corrected, healed, and transfigured.

To the modern mind, it is the nature of 'firsts' to reside in the past. In the Twentieth Century imagination they reside *down* in memory—specifically in the unconscious. Thus the term "depth psychology" is used to define those therapies that arise out of the philosophical premise that all therapeutic remedies ultimately derive from incursions into the past via the deep unconscious. When we speak of depth in psychology, we speak of a therapeutic setting in which the past, at some point (if not at all points), is the touchstone. The therapist sees, contemplates, measures, and decides upon the nature and personality of the client within the context of the client's past, always holding up to him the therapeutic image of an idyllic past—a should-have-been-past—that would have allowed the client to have experienced the present "normally," without psychological conflict. Here we again see the past cast in a psychotherapeutic cloak as the matrix of the thing called normality. The therapeutic move is always one that aims to correct, adjust, cure, the imperfect past that has given birth to the imperfect present. The client is therefore always located in a self-made Kali Yuga, a state of fallen grace, by virtue of the idea that his conflict has its origin in a flawed past that has robbed him of his inherent right to a present golden age. The unpredictable flow of events as a constancy in Being becomes defined as pathological in that childhood (or any time designated as the source of affliction) did not originate out of the dynamic urges of the original and ideal self.

Even more blind are those therapies that hang their hats upon the thesis that the expressed pathologies of an individual have their origin in the parent-child relationship. They overlook (or are ignorant of) the fact that the symptom can only be understood by a reconstruction of the values that produced it. Such values must not be construed as isolated in the parent-child relationship, but must instead look beyond this socially contrived structure. The parent-child relationship is but one of the configurations of a value system concerned with the literal creation of a person. The tendency of therapy to "adjust" the individual to a consideration and eventual egalitarian acceptance of the dynamics of this configuration is nothing less than a failure to discern why the archetype of the family has come about in the first place. Every image of the family, in every culture, is but the microcosmic presentation of the relationship of forces that occur on an everyday basis in the group where the family is located. The family is the site for the propagation of values, a clinic where what is wrong with the group becomes personified by the persons of the family, the identified patients.

In other words, the Western approach to actions determined inconsistent with a group's consensual agreement regarding appropriate social behavior has its source in our linear concept of genealogy—whose site is the family. The family is the place where the individual first experiences the manner by which the distribution of rights and power is determined by the status of persons (i.e., male/female, father/mother, brother/sister, older/younger, larger/smaller, stronger/weaker, etc.) shaped by social values. The behavior of each family member becomes identified as an expression of the family's ability or inability to transmit and maintain such distinctions.[228] The success of such transmission in the West rests upon the self-policing of the individual inaugurated by the idea of hereditary guilt. As E. R. Dodds stressed, the Western transition from a shame to a guilt culture is exemplified by the fact that in the earlier Homeric perspective the discovery of Oedipus' incest had little or no effect on the remainder of his life—not only did Oedipus continue his reign of Thebes, but went on to die a hero's death in battle, in the end buried with full and royal honors. It was only after the transition of Greece from a shame to a guilt culture that we then find the Sophoclean image of an Oedipus as "a polluted outcast, crushed under the burden of guilt 'which neither the earth nor the holy rain nor the sunlight can accept.'"[229] The hereditary fatedness of the Sophoclean Oedipus is that mirrored in modern psychology's description of the individual. That this of all possible stories was chosen by Freud to describe *any* facet of the psyche's operations tells us more about the power of archetypes as institutional directives and stories than about the psyche.

---

[228]cf. Plato, *Theaetetus* 173d and Republic 364bc.

[229]E. R. Dodds, *The Greeks and the Irrational*, Berkeley & Los Angeles: University of California Press, 1968, p. 36.

The Western marriage of genealogical linearity with the concept of hereditary guilt lies behind the modern definition of the symptom, which is in turn discussed in terms of patriarchal and matriarchal origins—of the family. What must be asked here is to what extent the Western definition of the "symptom" is shaped by a lineal arrangement of experience, to the sorting of experience and social reality in terms of linearity? To what extent is the Western symptom itself *symptomatic* (rather than an outcome) of patrilineal and matrileneal conceptualizations? Other more "primitive" cultures assign symptomatology to factors residing outside of the family—to spirits, demons, and curses, or what we might identify as the personification of social power and interaction rather than familial contagion. Evans-Pritchard (among others) alerted us to the existence of other forms of "lineage" in his observations of the Nuer. What the Nuer described as a lineage system, a genealogy, was actually "relations between groups of kinsmen within local communities rather than as a tree of descent, for the persons after whom the lineages are called do not all proceed from a single individual."[230] He adds that in illustrating this type of lineage system one must not chart it as a "series of bifurcation of descent, as a tree of descent, or as a series of triangles of ascent, but as a number of lines running at angles from a common point."[231]

In other words, any system of symptomatology based upon the Western genealogical perspective obfuscates the degree to which other and more immediate factors in the individual's cultural and social environment may be the source of his distress. It locates the individual in an essentially irremediable fate—the status of his ancestors— making of him a hostage to the redemptive techniques fashioned out of the very values that have given rise to the idea of such fatedness in the first place.

---

[230]Evans-Pritchard, *The Nuer,* Oxford: Clarendon Press, 1940, p. 202.
[231]*Ibid.*

iv.

If we understand consciousness as being but an organ of the psyche, rather than the psyche's representative, then we cannot think of its "development" or growth any more than one can speak of the development or growth of one's leg beyond its functional expression. It, as such an appendage, expresses itself functionally. If it must be thought of as an organ that "grows" or "develops," then there must be a point beyond which any organ cannot (or should not) pass beyond if it is to effectively fulfill its function. That is, one cannot develop a leg to the point where it supplants the functions of the body's other limbs without creating a monster. As the leg is limited by its own nature—to be a leg—so must consciousness be understood. Thus, consciousness as an organ can only develop to a point of useful functionality.

We have been manipulating the function of this organ: extending, shaping, organizing, strengthening, etc. consciousness, presuming in the first place that it is the whole of being, and on the other presuming that the necessary task is that of attending to its enhancement. That it is an extremely fragile organ must finally be accepted: it is its very nature, the limits of itself. By attempting to make of consciousness something that it isn't, we overlook the issues even its limited expression should most be attending to. Instead of attempting to make of consciousness a value, we should instead attempt to discover of what aid it is in a continued investigation into the source of values themselves. Even the most cursory review of history—which we in the West too often point to as the march of progress, equating it with some lubricious growth of consciousness—would reveal how little we have attended to this matter. One cannot isolate or divorce the presence and activity of consciousness in the midst of the historical flow of systems and values that have allowed (if not inaugurated) the perpetuation of inequities through the imposition of moralities. If this is the best that consciousness as a valued principle can do, then we should take another look at it.

As Jung had predicted, we have developed a cult of consciousness[232]—a narcissistic and cartographical involvement with psychic

---

[232]Jung, *CW*, vol. 13, para. 51.

domains that are not *even* fictions (elegantly constructed and engaging), but the wind of the wing of imagination, the flutterings of endless journal-writing, dream-recording, conversations with imaginal others, and active imaginations cementing the dissociative space between people to create monuments of elitist complacency passed off as transformations, as (even) actual events.

The intention of psychology had been to create a field of inquiry that sought to understand objectively the workings of the human psyche, proceeding from the assumption that its basic theoretical positions were value-free. As we have seen, such is not the case. Instead, the value-laden assumptions of early Greek thought have not only given shape to the field, but its impetus as well. All and every attempt to redefine, realign, revise, or reposition psychotherapeutic concerns since Freud's and Jung's original construction of the field must be understood as unsatisfactory, if not illusory. It is not enough to shuffle the particulars of the psychotherapeutic frame into new and interesting variations on a theme; it is not enough to claim the creation of a new method if that method has not first sought to question the validity of the original premise of depth psychology—that consciousness and the unconscious are known factors, the proper understanding and working of simply demanding continued interpretation. Such attempts are nothing more than the product of imagination and not the result of concerned philosophic inquiry. At most they are attempts at sophisticated intellectual entertainment that evade the demanding issues of immediate and social realities, pandering to a new star-system, a rock-and-roll tour promising salvation somewhere between an evening lecture and an all-day workshop.

We can no longer afford the leisure and celebration of such pastimes, but must instead attend to why it is (at such a perilous moment in history) we turn to such techniques and entertainments (as our ancestors have repeatedly done), and expect that things should turn out any different for us?, why at the very moment of crisis we call upon the powers of an ultimate reality which if it truly existed would have to be called to task for having brought us to this juncture in the first place?

V.

As I had suggested in Part II, the Twentieth-Century self (or ego) is defined by and emerges from the interstice created by the overlapping folds of the three socially constructed persons that constitute what we refer to as the "individual." These three persons, composed of the values determining rights of inclusion and exclusion (and therefore personifications of social powers), might be thought of as generating a field of force arising out of the polarized valuations they each embody. Folded upon one another as if they were a child's pick-up sticks haphazardly thrown, the three persons creating the interstice form a field generated by the disparities existing between each of them.

The individual, a composite of the polarized values embodying these three persons, knits itself together through a process of selection, mediation, revision, and adaptation. Whereas the social, cultural, and metaphysical persons tend to be composed of institutional values, thereby attaining constancy (if not fixity), the individual is affected by a chance factor missing in the three persons. That is, the individual is also a composite of the diversities arising among the three. Choice, chance, and circumstance ultimately determine in what way the three socially constructed persons will find agreement (or a modicum of adjustment) with one another in the figure of the individual, who is in turn lifted from the interstice as the potter pulls his form up from the wheel. This is the source of the quantum we refer to as ego-consciousness.

Consciousness is not only contoured by the values of the three persons, it is a function created and shaped by them. The prominence of the values of one person over the others at any given time changes the shape of this interstice they equally share. In the final analysis consciousness is an ephemeral organ—a function and not a thing in itself. As a "subject", it "is not something that creates effects, but only a fiction."[233]

---

[233]Friedrich Nietzsche, *The Will to Power,* Walter Kaufmann and R. J. Hollingdale, trans., New York: Vintage Books, 1968, Book III, sec. 552., p. 297.

The individual initially created in this manner, an individual who *identifies* himself with consciousness, thinking it is an attribute rather than a function, is himself but a function. He is a sign in a system of values. Because the collective unconscious is an image of the world, and the archetypes are located in the collective unconscious, we must then assume that this image *qua* image is a photographic statement. The image, as the photograph, shows us the thing itself: everything that can be said about the archetypes correctly represents the relationships between and within the institutions they personify. What we have failed to understand is that the archetypal image is but an aesthetic studio-portrait of the thing itself. The photo-image does not precede the thing it is an image of. What the archetypes represent are not gods, but the personification of our justification to act as if we were gods. The archetypes (or the gods) are our permission to be as ourselves, the justification to utterly disregard the intent of the values we not only live by, but seek to impose upon others as well. The archetypes (and the gods) exist only within the bounded dimension of the natural attitude, which must perforce (because of the social sequencing of the foldings) initially give coherence to the interstice. It is for this reason that consciousness and the natural attitude are generally assumed to be synonymous. The language that constitutes the consciousness of the natural attitude is utilitarian, as is the consciousness it has given rise to. It is the language of the natural attitude as conveyed by the three persons—the language of an emptiness, a nightwatchman making his rounds.

We have seen that language precedes consciousness, arising out of the need to communicate. But the language that first arises out of this need must be understood as a first-order language. It is only employed to communicate a need. That is, the consciousness of the natural attitude, coming into existence to convey and address needs, is a semiology of needs. The natural attitude is a condition of lack, and the consciousness that exemplifies it is the personification of its want. The story of the Socratic Eros portrays this condition by making of his father plenty, and his mother lack or need.[234] The desire for plenty expressed from a place of need is

---

[234]Plato, *Symposium*, 203b, ff.

not only our image of Love (and here I refer you to the psycho-analytic idea that the transference is a "love" situation), but that by which we seek to bind ourselves to one another. This lack which seeks plenty lies behind the creation of the idea of wholeness—which presupposes a condition of lack within each of us. It is this imagination which therapy presently feeds when it informs us that what we must enthusiastically seek to resuscitate is an original psychic unity.

What this suggests is that it is only by giving up this idea of an *a priori* wholeness that we can ever free ourselves from the illusion of lack and the absence of being. If there is any one truth, it is the expression of continued becoming. An *a priori* self or wholeness, because of its repetitious re-enactment, demands the exclusion of diversities and differences, of meaningless chance and the ensuing free creative responses to chance that allows a continuing inspection and permutation of values, rather than the perpetuation of those values concretized by the *a priori*. The identification of therapeutic concerns with the millennial construction of the *a priori* self serves effectively to short-circuit the natural outreach of becoming. It aids in the creation and maintenance of the Breugelian consciousness that presently shapes and defines Western consensual reality; a consciousness illuminated by the inflation of fallen angels—the forgotten returned as a higher value. It is inevitable that a consciousness constructed of guilt and self-recriminations will in time distribute ills in the name of conversion, salvation, and transformation. Becoming so truncated collapses into a replica of appearances, the demand of norms. Creativity is given up in favor of consistency.

What is demanded is a therapy that does not approach the psyche from the value system of need—one which would no longer seek the past, moving away from the present and the future, to resuscitate forgotten memories so that they might be assigned meaning and appended as mortar to the permeable membrane of consciousness. Such a therapy would not seek to turn the self into a reformed amnesiac, a suffering memory regurgitated in the name of growth. It would instead question the values that gave birth to the idea that the forgotten leads to the future, that what has already been suffered must be resurfaced, that the pillars of salt the backward glance creates are grains of wisdom. It would bring an end to the type of consciousness composed of suffering as the keystone of transformation.

If language is what gives rise to consciousness, then we are in need of another language if we expect to move beyond the socially utilitarian consciousness of the natural attitude. The space that therapy should seek is one where the ruse of interpretation has been scraped out, where this looking beneath, seeing through, this deepening of depth psychology which insists that the surface of things is not enough if we are to understand, comes to an end; where this belief that the truth may only be discovered by the continued discovery of links in a long chain of associations, of memory assigned to an assembly line of connections, comes to an end.

vi.

If understanding is only to be arrived at through the interpretation of the symbolic underpinnings of history (i.e., Freud's latent content), then the apparent and visible surface of things (the manifest content) must always be undermined. All interpretation moves us away from the visible and apparent in its move towards what we are told is the truth—a truth predetermined by whichever therapeutic story it is that seeks to convert the opacity of acts into a transparency of image.

If it is only within latency where the truth is to be found, then the manifest can be nothing more than a lie, a fiction. The consciousness that the patient brings to therapy will always be received as invalid in that it exists as something that must be adjusted. It is implied that the therapist must discover what is "wrong" with this consciousness, and by so doing automatically implies that there is a truth to be discovered which the individual himself does not know. From this standpoint, if the unconscious contains the truth, then consciousness is fictive. And the proof, the Q.E.D. that the truth has been found will be the "discovery" of the true story. As we have seen this therapeutic story is the product of the therapist's prodding of the patient's memory into newly discovered strata—strata where a psychological meaning will substantiate the presence of malignancy. The fictive nature of the patient is brought to truth by the invagination of the therapist's Institutional story produced as the patient's own.

But what if what we are looking for in such *under*-standings lies immediately in the shadows of the surface, hidden in the opacity of acts, gestures, statements that psychology perpetually treats as if they are windows separating us from pure meaning? By continually looking beneath and behind the act, psychology depersonalizes the act. It assures us that if the act is to have any meaning it must disclose a history, lead to a multiplicity of meanings subtly engineered by interpretation. We must bring your mother, father, brother, friend, lover into this if we are to understand why you beat your wife, have a passion for the instep of women's shoes, care nothing for your life, or think and find yourself mad. You as your own significator are not enough. A fine linen of meaning must be wrapped around your story to keep it together. Only in time might one discover that what finally holds one together in this setting is the very thing one had hoped to free oneself from—a possession. You discover that you have achieved an immortalizing state of wholeness by a withdrawal of a fear that had been imposed upon you from the outset—that there is something wrong. To be cured of this wrong is to actually never be freed of it for now you have become something (the cured one, the analyzed one) *because* of it. Here one becomes other-than-oneself. One becomes transfigured, an eternal convert to the horizon of a likely story.

January 1990
San Francisco